The Merry Wives of Windsor

The Merry Wives of Windsor

William Shakespeare

Illustrated by
Hugh Thomson

Gramercy Books
New York • Avenel

Preface and Compilation
Copyright © 1995 by Random House Value Publishing, Inc.

This 1995 edition is published by Gramercy Books,
distributed by Random House Value Publishing, Inc.,
40 Engelhard Avenue
Avenel, New Jersey 07001

Random House
New York • Toronto • London • Sydney • Auckland

Printed and bound in Singapore

Library of Congress Cataloging-in-Publication Data
Shakespeare, William, 1564-1616.
The merry wives of Windsor / William Shakespeare ;
illustrated by Hugh Thomson.
p. cm.
ISBN 0-517-12220-0
1. Falstaff, John, Sir (Fictitious character)—Drama.
2. Married women—England—Windsor—Drama. I. Title.
PR2826.A1 1995
822.3'3—dc20   94-24673
                                                            CIP

8 7 6 5 4 3 2 1

Preface

William Shakespeare's Falstaff, that shrewd and ever mischievous lord of misrule who grandly inhabits the two *Henry IV* plays, is one of his greatest comic creations. He is a complex and mythic composite of the figure of Vice from the old morality plays and the liberating Fool, who rails against convention and restraint. Falstaff's popularity was so great that Queen Elizabeth is said to have commanded Shakespeare to write a play portraying Falstaff in love. The result was *The Merry Wives of Windsor*, which he reportedly wrote in fourteen days.

The Merry Wives of Windsor was probably written in 1597. This play has no known specific source for its plot. It is perhaps Shakespeare's lightest comedy and also his most realistic. Unlike his other comedies it is uniquely English in setting and character. The language is colloquial and littered with allusions to contemporary middle-class life that anyone in Elizabethan London would have recognized.

The story revolves around the farcical attempts of the amoral and lecherous Falstaff to seduce two women, Mistress Page and Mistress Ford. In spirit, the comedy derives from the Italian tradition of the *fabliau*, or tale of sexual misadventure, that Shakespeare was well familiar with. But unlike the traditional *fabliau*, Falstaff, the lover, is extremely unsuccessful since he is foiled by the chaste women who resourcefully outsmart him. In one notable scene, for example, Falstaff ignobly hides from an irate husband in a heap of wet wash.

It has often been said that the Falstaff of *The Merry Wives of Windsor* is not as memorable as he was in his earlier incarnation in *Henry IV*. The eminent Shakespearean critic A.C. Bradley went so far as to call the Falstaff of *Merry Wives* an "impostor." William Hazlitt, another well-known critic, wrote that Falstaff and the other characters that return here—Mistress Quickly, Nym, Bardolph, and Shallow—are "but the shadows of what they were." It is certainly difficult to imagine the relatively ingenuous Mistress Page capable of deceiving the sharply witty and conniving Falstaff of *Henry IV*. Some critics have argued that Shakespeare, because he had taken the character as far as he could artistically, was not interested in his creation any longer, and it was only a royal decree that forced him to resurrect Falstaff who he killed off in *Henry V*.

But, nevertheless, the play, is a delightful and lively comedy, which, when taken on its own merits, is extremely entertaining. As Hazlitt says, "*The Merry Wives of Windsor* is a very amusing play, with a great deal of humor, character, and nature in it." A perennial favorite among audiences, the play even became the basis for Guiseppe Verdi's final opera, *Falstaff*.

Shakespeare's plays were first published individually, in Quarto editions. Later they were collected and published in Folio editions. There are often variations in the text from edition to edition. The text of this edition of *The Merry Wives of Windsor* is the nearest possible approximation to what Shakespeare actually wrote and is based on the earliest reliable printed texts. To avoid distraction, however, the spelling has been modernized. Where a Quarto text exists as well as the First Folio, the passages which occur only in the Quarto are enclosed in square brackets and those which occur only in the Folio are enclosed in brace brackets. The punctuation adheres closely to the Elizabethan punctuation of the early texts and, therefore, is often indicative of the way in which the lines are to be spoken.

This beautiful edition of *The Merry Wives of Windsor* was illustrated by Hugh Thomson, who imaginatively captures its comic qualities as well as the ambience of Elizabethan England.

CHRISTOPHER MOORE

New York
1995

Dramatis Personae

SIR JOHN FALSTAFF.
FENTON, *a gentleman.*
SHALLOW, *a country justice.*
SLENDER, *cousin to Shallow.*
FORD, ⎫
PAGE, ⎬ *two gentlemen dwelling at Windsor.*
WILLIAM PAGE, *a boy, son to Page.*
SIR HUGH EVANS, *a Welsh parson.*
DOCTOR CAIUS, *a French physician.*
Host of the Garter Inn.
BARDOLPH, ⎫
PISTOL, ⎬ *sharpers attending on Falstaff.*
NYM, ⎭
ROBIN, *page to Falstaff.*
SIMPLE, *servant to Slender.*
RUGBY, *servant to Doctor Caius.*

MISTRESS FORD.
MISTRESS PAGE.
ANNE PAGE, *her daughter.*
MISTRESS QUICKLY, *servant to Doctor Caius.*

Servants to Page, Ford, etc.

SCENE: *Windsor, and the neighbourhood.*

Act I

Scene 1

Windsor. Before Page's house

Enter Justice Shallow, Slender, and Sir Hugh Evans

Shallow. Sir Hugh, persuade me not; I will make a Star-chamber matter of it, if he were twenty Sir John Fal-staffs, he shall not abuse Robert Shallow, esquire.

Slender. In the county of Gloucester, justice of peace and 'Coram.'

Shallow. Ay, cousin Slender, and 'Custalorum.'

Slender. Ay, and 'Ratolorum' too; and a gentleman born, master parson, who writes himself 'Armigero,' in any bill, warrant, quittance, or obligation, 'Armigero.'

Shallow. Ay, that I do, and have done any time these three hundred years.

Slender. All his successors (gone before him) hath done 't; and all his ancestors (that come after him) may: they may give the dozen white luces in their coat.

Shallow. It is an old coat.

Evans. The dozen white louses do become an old coat well; it agrees well, passant; it is a familiar beast to man, and signifies love.

Shallow. The luce is the fresh fish; the salt fish is an old coat.

Slender. I may quarter, coz.

Shallow. You may, by marrying.

Evans. It is marring indeed, if he quarter it.

Shallow. Not a whit.

Evans. Yes, py'r lady; if he has a quarter of your coat, there is but three skirts for yourself, in my simple conjectures: but that is all one. If Sir John Falstaff have committed disparagements unto you, I am of the church, and will be glad to do my benevolence, to make atonements and compremises between you.

Shallow. The council shall hear it, it is a riot.

Evans. It is not meet the council hear a riot; there is no fear of Got in a riot: the council (look you) shall desire to hear the fear of Got, and not to hear a riot; take your vizaments in that.

Shallow. Ha! o' my life, if I were young again, the sword should end it.

Evans. It is petter that friends is the sword, and end it: and there is also another device in my prain, which peradventure prings goot discretions with it:—there is Anne Page, which is daughter to Master Thomas Page, which is pretty virginity.

Slender. Mistress Anne Page? She has brown hair, and speaks small like a woman.

Evans. It is that fery person for all the 'orld, as just as you will desire; and seven hundred pounds of moneys, and gold, and silver, is her grandsire upon his death's-bed (Got deliver to a joyful resurrections!) give, when she is able to overtake seventeen years old: it were a goot motion if we leave our pribbles and prabbles, and desire a marriage between Master Abraham and Mistress Anne Page.

Slender. Did her grandsire leave her seven hundred pound?

Evans. Ay, and her father is make her a petter penny.

Slender. I know the young gentlewoman, she has good gifts.

Evans. Seven hundred pounds, and possibilities, is goot gifts.

Shallow. Well, let us see honest Master Page. Is Falstaff there?

Evans. Shall I tell you a lie? I do despise a liar, as I do despise one that is false, or as I despise one that is not true. The knight, Sir John, is there; and, I beseech you, be ruled by your well-willers. I will peat the door for Master Page. (*Knocks.*) What, hoa! Got pless your house here!

Page. (*within*) Who's there?

Enter Page

Evans. Here is Got's plessing and your friend, and Justice Shallow, and here young Master Slender; that peradventures shall tell you another tale, if matters grow to your likings.

Page. I am glad to see your worships well. I thank you for my venison, Master Shallow.

Shallow. Master Page, I am glad to see you: much good do it your good heart! I wish'd your venison better, it was ill kill'd. How doth good Mistress Page?—and I thank you always with my heart, la! with my heart.

Page. Sir, I thank you.

Shallow. Sir, I thank you; by yea and no, I do.

Page. I am glad to see you, good Master Slender.

Slender. How does your fallow greyhound, sir? I heard say he was outrun on Cotsall.

Page. It could not be judg'd, sir.

Slender. You'll not confess, you'll not confess.

Shallow. That he will not, 'tis your fault, 'tis your fault; 'tis a good dog.

Page. A cur, sir.

Shallow. Sir, he's a good dog, and a fair dog, can there be more said? he is good and fair. Is Sir John Falstaff here?

Page. Sir, he is within; and I would I could do a good office between you.

Evans. It is spoke as a Christians ought to speak.

Shallow. He hath wrong'd me, Master Page.

Page. Sir, he doth in some sort confess it.

Shallow. If it be confessed, it is not redressed: is not that so, Master Page? He hath wrong'd me, indeed he hath, at a

word: he hath, believe me Robert Shallow, esquire, saith
he is wrong'd.

Page. Here comes Sir John.

Enter Sir John Falstaff, Bardolph, Nym, and Pistol

Falstaff. Now, Master Shallow, you'll complain of me to the
king?

Shallow. Knight, you have beaten my men, killed my deer,
and broke open my lodge.

Falstaff. But not kiss'd your keeper's daughter?

Shallow. Tut, a pin! this shall be answer'd.

Falstaff. I will answer it straight, I have done all this:
That is now answer'd.

Shallow. The council shall know this.

Falstaff. 'Twere better for you if it were known in counsel:
you'll be laugh'd at.

Evans. *Pauca verba,* Sir John; goot worts.

Falstaff. Good worts? good cabbage. Slender, I broke your
head: what matter have you against me?

Slender. Marry, sir, I have matter in my head against you,
and against your cony-catching rascals, Bardolph, Nym,
and Pistol. [They carried me to the tavern and made me
drunk, and afterward pick'd my pocket.]

Bardolph. You Banbury cheese!

Slender. Ay, it is no matter.

Pistol. How now, Mephostophilus?

Slender. Ay, it is no matter.

Nym. Slice, I say! *pauca, pauca:* slice! that's my humour.

Slender. Where's Simple, my man? Can you tell, cousin?

Evans. Peace, I pray you; now let us understand. There is
three umpires in this matter, as I understand; that is, Master Page (fidelicet Master Page), and there is myself
(fidelicet myself), and the three party is (lastly, and fi-
nally) mine host of the Garter.

Page. We three to hear it, and end it between them.

Evans. Fery goot, I will make a prief of it in my note-book;

and we will afterwards 'ork upon the cause, with as great discreetly as we can.

Falstaff. Pistol!

Pistol. He hears with ears.

Evans. The tevil and his tam! what phrase is this? 'He hears with ear'? why, it is affectations.

Falstaff. Pistol, did you pick Master Slender's purse?

Slender. Ay, by these gloves did he, or I would I might never come in mine own great chamber again else, of seven groats in mill-sixpences, and two Edward shovel-boards, that cost me two shilling and two pence a-piece of Yead Miller: by these gloves.

Falstaff. Is this true, Pistol?

Evans. No, it is false, if it is a pick-purse.

Pistol. Ha, thou mountain-foreigner! Sir John, and master mine,

I combat challenge of this latten bilbo.

Word of denial in thy *labras* here!

Word of denial: froth and scum, thou liest!

Slender. By these gloves, then, 'twas he.

Nym. Be avis'd, sir, and pass good humours: I will say 'marry trap' with you, if you run the nuthook's humour on me, that is the very note of it.

Slender. By this hat, then he in the red face had it; for though I cannot remember what I did when you made me drunk, yet I am not altogether an ass.

Falstaff. What say you, Scarlet, and John?

Bardolph. Why, sir, for my part, I say the gentleman had drunk himself out of his five sentences.

Evans. It is his five senses: fie, what the ignorance is!

Bardolph. And being fap, sir, was (as they say) cashier'd; and so conclusions passed the careires.

Slender. Ay, you spake in Latin then too; but 'tis no matter: I'll ne'er be drunk whilst I live again, but in honest, civil, godly company, for this trick: if I be drunk, I'll be drunk with those that have the fear of God, and not with drunken knaves.

Evans. So Got 'udge me, that is a virtuous mind.

Falstaff. You hear all these matters denied, gentlemen; you hear it.

Enter Anne Page, with wine; Mistress Ford and Mistress Page, following

Page. Nay, daughter, carry the wine in, we'll drink within.

Exit Anne Page

Slender. O heaven! this is Mistress Anne Page.

Page. How now, Mistress Ford?

Falstaff. Mistress Ford, by my troth you are very well met: by your leave, good mistress.   *Kisses her*

Page. Wife, bid these gentlemen welcome. Come, we have a hot venison pasty to dinner: come, gentlemen, I hope we shall drink down all unkindness.

Exeunt all except Shallow, Slender, and Evans

Slender. I had rather than forty shillings I had my Book of Songs and Sonnets here.

Enter Simple

How now, Simple, where have you been? I must wait on myself, must I? You have not the Book of Riddles about you, have you?

Simple. Book of Riddles? why, did you not lend it to Alice Shortcake upon All-hallowmas last, a fortnight afore Michaelmas?

Shallow. Come coz, come coz, we stay for you: a word with you, coz; marry this, coz: there is as 'twere a tender, a kind of tender, made afar off by Sir Hugh here. Do you understand me?

Slender. Ay, sir, you shall find me reasonable; if it be so, I shall do that that is reason.

Shallow. Nay, but understand me.

Slender. So I do, sir.

Evans. Give ear to his motions; Master Slender, I will description the matter to you, if you be capacity of it.

Slender. Nay, I will do as my cousin Shallow says: I pray you pardon me, he's a justice of peace in his country, simple though I stand here.

Evans. But that is not the question: the question is concerning your marriage.

Shallow. Ay, there's the point, sir.

Evans. Marry, is it; the very point of it, to Mistress Anne Page.

Slender. Why, if it be so, I will marry her upon any reasonable demands.

Evans. But can you affection the 'oman? let us command to know that of your mouth, or of your lips; for divers philosophers hold that the lips is parcel of the mouth. Therefore precisely, can you carry your good will to the maid?

Shallow. Cousin Abraham Slender, can you love her?

Slender. I hope, sir, I will do as it shall become one that would do reason.

Evans. Nay, Got's lords, and his ladies! you must speak possitable, if you can carry-her your desires towards her.

Shallow. That you must. Will you (upon good dowry) marry her?

Slender. I will do a greater thing than that, upon your request, cousin, in any reason.

Shallow. Nay, conceive me, conceive me, sweet coz: what I do is to pleasure you, coz: can you love the maid?

Slender. I will marry her, sir, at your request: but if there be no great love in the beginning, yet heaven may decrease it upon better acquaintance, when we are married, and have more occasion to know one another: I hope upon familiarity will grow more content: but if you say 'Marry her,' I will marry her; that I am freely dissolved, and dissolutely.

Evans. It is a fery discretion-answer; save the fall is in the ord 'dissolutely': the 'ort is, according to our meaning, 'resolutely': his meaning is good.

Shallow. Ay, I think my cousin meant well.

Slender. Ay, or else I would I might be hang'd, la!

Shallow. Here comes fair Mistress Anne.

Re-enter Anne Page

Would I were young for your sake, Mistress Anne!

Anne. The dinner is on the table, my father desires your worships' company.

Shallow. I will wait on him, fair Mistress Anne.

Evans. Od's plessed-will! I will not be absence at the grace.

Exeunt Shallow and Evans

Anne. Will 't please your worship to come in, sir?

Slender. No, I thank you forsooth, heartily; I am very well.

Anne. The dinner attends you, sir.

Slender. I am not a-hungry, I thank you, forsooth. Go, sirrah, for all you are my man, go wait upon my cousin Shallow. (*exit Simple.*) A justice of peace sometime may be beholding to his friend, for a man; I keep but three men and a boy yet, till my mother be dead: but what though? yet I live like a poor gentleman born.

Anne. I may not go in without your worship: they will not sit till you come.

Slender. I' faith, I'll eat nothing; I thank you as much as though I did.

Anne. I pray you, sir, walk in.

Slender. I had rather walk here, I thank you. I bruis'd my shin th' other day with playing at sword and dagger with a master of fence (three veneys for a dish of stew'd prunes) [and I with my ward defending my head, he hot my shin,] and, by my troth, I cannot abide the smell of hot meat since. Why do your dogs bark so? be there bears i' the town?

Anne. I think there are, sir, I heard them talk'd of.

Slender. I love the sport well, but I shall as soon quarrel at

it, as any man in England. You are afraid if you see the
bear loose, are you not?

Anne. Ay, indeed, sir.

Slender. That's meat and drink to me, now: I have seen
Sackerson loose, twenty times, and have taken him by the
chain; but, I warrant you, the women have so cried and
shriek'd at it, that it pass'd: but women, indeed, cannot
abide 'em, they are very ill-favour'd rough things.

Re-enter Page

Page. Come, gentle Master Slender, come; we stay for you.

Slender. I'll eat nothing, I thank you, sir.

Page. By cock and pie, you shall not choose, sir! come,
come.

Slender. Nay, pray you lead the way.

Page. Come on, sir.

Slender. Mistress Anne, yourself shall go first.

Anne. Not I, sir; pray you keep on.

Slender. Truly, I will not go first; truly, la! I will not do you
that wrong.

Anne. I pray you, sir.

Slender. I'll rather be unmannerly than troublesome. You
do yourself wrong, indeed, la!   *Exeunt*

Scene II

Enter Sir Hugh Evans and Simple

Evans. Go your ways, and ask of Doctor Caius' house which is the way: and there dwells one Mistress Quickly; which is in the manner of his nurse; or his try nurse; or his cook; or his laundry; his washer, and his wringer.

Simple. Well, sir.

Evans. Nay, it is petter yet. Give her this letter; for it is a 'oman that altogether's acquaintance with Mistress Anne Page; and the letter is to desire and require her to solicit your master's desires, to Mistress Anne Page. I pray you, be gone: I will make an end of my dinner; there's pippins and cheese to come.   *Exeunt*

Scene III

A room in the Garter Inn

Enter Falstaff, Host, Bardolph, Nym, Pistol, and Robin

Falstaff. Mine host of the Garter!

Host. What says my bully-rook? speak scholarly, and wisely.

Falstaff. Truly, mine host; I must turn away some of my followers.

Host. Discard, bully Hercules, cashier; let them wag; trot, trot.

Falstaff. I sit at ten pounds a week.

Host. Thou 'rt an emperor, Cæsar, Keisar, and Pheezar. I will entertain Bardolph; he shall draw; he shall tap: said I well, bully Hector?

Falstaff. Do so, good mine host.

Host. I have spoke; let him follow. (*to Bardolph*) Let me see thee froth and lime: I am at a word; follow.   *Exit*

Falstaff. Bardolph, follow him: a tapster is a good trade: an old cloak makes a new jerkin; a wither'd servingman a fresh tapster. Go, adieu.

Bardolph. It is a life that I have desir'd: I will thrive.

Pistol. O base Hungarian wight! wilt thou the spigot wield?
                              Exit Bardolph

Nym. He was gotten in drink: [his mind is not heroic: and there's the humour of it:] is not the humour conceited?

Falstaff. I am glad I am so acquit of this tinder-box: his thefts were too open; his filching was like an unskilful singer, he kept not time.

Nym. The good humour is to steal at a minute's rest.

Pistol. 'Convey,' the wise it call. 'Steal?' foh! a fico for the phrase!

Falstaff. Well, sirs, I am almost out at heels.

Pistol. Why then let kibes ensue.

Falstaff. There is no remedy; I must cony-catch, I must shift.

Pistol. Young ravens must have food.

Falstaff. Which of you know Ford of this town?

Pistol. I ken the wight: he is of substance good.

Falstaff. My honest lads, I will tell you what I am about—

Pistol. Two yards, and more.

Falstaff. No quips now, Pistol! (Indeed, I am in the waist two yards about; but I am now about no waste; I am about thrift) briefly: I do mean to make love to Ford's wife: I spy entertainment in her; she discourses; she carves; she gives the leer of invitation: I can construe the action of her familiar style, and the hardest voice of her behaviour (to be English'd rightly) is, 'I am Sir John Falstaff's.'

Pistol. He hath studied her will; and translated her will; out of honesty, into English.

Nym. The anchor is deep: will that humour pass?

Falstaff. Now, the report goes she has all the rule of her husband's purse: he hath a legend of angels.

Pistol. As many devils entertain; and 'To her, boy,' say I.

Nym. The humour rises; it is good: humour me the angels.

Falstaff. I have writ me here a letter to her: and here another to Page's wife, who even now gave me good eyes too; examin'd my parts with most judicious œillades; sometimes the beam of her view gilded my foot, sometimes my portly belly.

Pistol. Then did the sun on dunghill shine.

Nym. I thank thee for that humour.

Falstaff. O, she did so course o'er my exteriors with such a greedy intention, that the appetite of her eye did seem to scorch me up like a burning-glass! Here's another letter to her: she bears the purse too; she is a region in Guiana; all gold and bounty. I will be cheaters to them both, and they shall be exchequers to me; they shall be my East and

West Indies, and I will trade to them both. Go, bear thou
this letter to Mistress Page; and thou this to Mistress
Ford: we will thrive, lads, we will thrive.

Pistol. Shall I Sir Pandarus of Troy become,
And by my side wear steel? then Lucifer take all!

Nym. I will run no base humour: here, take the humour-
letter: I will keep the haviour of reputation.

Falstaff. (*to Robin*) Hold, sirrah, bear you these letters
tightly,
Sail like my pinnace to these golden shores.
Rogues, hence, avaunt, vanish like hailstones, go;
Trudge; plod away o' the hoof; seek shelter, pack!
Falstaff will learn the humour of the age,
French thrift, you rogues, myself, and skirted Page.

Exeunt Falstaff and Robin

Pistol. Let vultures gripe thy guts! for gourd and fullam
holds,
And high and low beguiles the rich and poor:
Tester I'll have in pouch when thou shalt lack,
Base Phrygian Turk!

Nym. I have operations, [in my head] which be humours
of revenge.

Pistol. Wilt thou revenge?

Nym. By Welkin, and her star!

Pistol. With wit, or steel?

Nym. With both the humours, I:
I will discuss the humour of this love to Page.

Pistol. And I to Ford shall eke unfold
How Falstaff (varlet vile)
His dove will prove, his gold will hold,
And his soft couch defile.

Nym. My humour shall not cool: I will incense Page to deal
with poison; I will possess him with yellows, for the revolt
of mine is dangerous: that is my true humour.

Pistol. Thou art the Mars of malecontents; I second thee;
troop on.   *Exeunt*

Scene IV

A room in Doctor Caius's house

Enter Mistress Quickly, Simple, and Rugby

Quickly. What, John Rugby? I pray thee, go to the casement, and see if you can see my master, Master Doctor Caius, coming. If he do, i' faith, and find anybody in the house, here will be an old abusing of God's patience, and the king's English.

Rugby. I'll go watch.

Quickly. Go, and we'll have a posset for 't soon at night, in faith, at the latter end of a sea-coal fire. (*exit Rugby.*) An honest, willing, kind fellow, as ever servant shall come in house withal; and I warrant you, no tell-tale, nor no breed-bate: his worst fault is, that he is given to prayer; he is something peevish that way; but nobody but has his fault; but let that pass. Peter Simple, you say your name is?

Simple. Ay; for fault of a better.

Quickly. And Master Slender's your master?

Simple. Ay, forsooth.

Quickly. Does he not wear a great round beard, like a glover's paring-knife?

Simple. No, forsooth: he hath but a little whey face; with a little yellow beard,—a cane-colour'd beard.

Quickly. A softly-sprighted man, is he not?

Simple. Ay, forsooth: but he is as tall a man of his hands as any is between this and his head; he hath fought with a warrener.

Quickly. How say you?—O, I should remember him: does he not hold up his head, as it were, and strut in his gait?

Simple. Yes, indeed, does he.

Quickly. Well, heaven send Anne Page no worse fortune!

Tell Master Parson Evans I will do what I can for your master: Anne is a good girl, and I wish—

Re-enter Rugby

Rugby. Out, alas! here comes my master.

Quickly. We shall all be shent. Run in here, good young man; go into this closet: he will not stay long. (*Shuts Simple in the closet.*) What, John Rugby! John! what, John, I say! Go, John, go inquire for my master, I doubt he be not well, that he comes not home.
(*singing*) And down, down, adown-a, etc.

Enter Doctor Caius

Caius. Vat is you sing? I do not like des toys. Pray you go and vetch me in my closet un boitier vert,—a box, a green-a-box: do intend vat I speak? a green-a-box.

Quickly. Ay, forsooth, I'll fetch it you. (*aside*) I am glad he went not in himself: if he had found the young man, he would have been horn-mad.

Caius. Fe, fe, fe, fe! ma foi, il fait fort chaud. Je m'en vais à la cour,—la grande affaire.

Quickly. Is it this, sir?

Caius. Oui; mette le au mon pocket: dépêche, quickly. Vere is dat knave Rugby?

Quickly. What, John Rugby! John!

Rugby. Here, Sir!

Caius. You are John Rugby, and you are Jack Rugby. Come, take-a your rapier, and come after my heel to the court.

Rugby. 'Tis ready, sir, here in the porch.

Caius. By my trot', I tarry too long. Od's me! Qu'ai-j'oublié? dere is some simples in my closet, dat I vill not for the varld I shall leave behind.

Quickly. Ay me, he'll find the young man there, and be mad!

Caius. O diable, diable! vat is in my closet? Villany! larron! (*Pulling Simple out.*) Rugby, my rapier!

Quickly. Good master, be content.

Caius. Wherefore shall I be content-a?

Quickly. The young man is an honest man.

Caius. What shall de honest man do in my closet? dere is no honest man dat shall come in my closet.

Quickly. I beseech you be not so phlegmatic: hear the truth of it: he came of an errand to me, from Parson Hugh.

Caius. Vell?

Simple. Ay, forsooth; to desire her to—

Quickly. Peace, I pray you.

Caius. Peace-a-your tongue. Speak-a-your tale.

Simple. To desire this honest gentlewoman, your maid, to speak a good word to Mistress Anne Page, for my master in the way of marriage.

Quickly. This is all, indeed, la! but I'll ne'er put my finger in the fire, and need not.

Caius. Sir Hugh send-a you? Rugby, baille me some paper. Tarry you a little-a-while. *Writes*

Quickly. (*aside to Simple*) I am glad he is so quiet: if he had been throughly mov'd, you should have heard him so loud and so melancholy. But notwithstanding, man, I'll do you your master what good I can: and the very yea and the no is, the French doctor, my master,—I may call him my master, look you, for I keep his house; and I wash, wring, brew, bake, scour, dress meat and drink, make the beds, and do all myself,—

Simple. (*aside to Mistress Quickly*) 'Tis a great charge to come under one body's hand.

Quickly. (*aside to Simple*) Are you avis'd o' that? you shall find it a great charge: and to be up early and down late;— but notwithstanding, (to tell you in your ear; I would have no words of it) my master himself is in love with Mistress Anne Page: but notwithstanding that I know Anne's mind, that's neither here nor there.

Caius. You, jack'nape; give-a this letter to Sir Hugh; by gar, it is a shallenge: I will cut his troat in de park, and I will teach a scurvy jack-a-nape priest to meddle, or make:—

you may be gone; it is not good you tarry here.—By gar,
I will cut all his two stones; by gar, he shall not have a
stone to throw at his dog.   *Exit Simple*

Quickly. Alas, he speaks but for his friend.

Caius. It is no matter-a ver dat:—do not you tell-a-me dat I
shall have Anne Page for myself? By gar, I vill kill de Jack
priest; and I have appointed mine host of de Jarteer to
measure our weapon.—By gar, I will myself have Anne
Page.

Quickly. Sir, the maid loves you, and all shall be well: we
must give folks leave to prate: what, the good-jer!

Caius. Rugby, come to the court with me. By gar, if I have
not Anne Page, I shall turn your head out of my door. Follow my heels, Rugby.   *Exeunt Caius and Rugby*

Quickly. You shall have An fool's-head of your own. No, I
know Anne's mind for that: never a woman in Windsor
knows more of Anne's mind than I do, nor can do more
than I do with her, I thank heaven.

Fenton. (*within*) Who's within there, ho?

Quickly. Who's there, I trow? Come near the house, I, pray
you.

Enter Fenton

Fenton. How now, good woman, how dost thou?

Quickly. The better that it pleases your good worship to ask.

Fenton. What news? how does pretty Mistress Anne?

Quickly. In truth, sir, and she is pretty, and honest, and gentle, and one that is your friend, I can tell you that by the
way; I praise heaven for it.

Fenton. Shall I do any good, think'st thou? Shall I not lose
my suit?

Quickly. Troth, sir, all is in his hands above: but notwithstanding, Master Fenton, I'll be sworn on a book she loves
you. Have not your worship a wart above your eye?

Fenton. Yes marry have I, what of that?

Quickly. Well, thereby hangs a tale;—good faith, it is such another Nan; but, I detest, an honest maid as ever broke bread:—we had an hour's talk of that wart.—I shall never laugh but in that maid's company!—But, indeed, she is given too much to allicholy and musing: but for you—well, go to.

Fenton. Well, I shall see her to-day: hold, there's money for thee; let me have thy voice in my behalf: if thou seest her before me, commend me.

Quickly. Will I? i' faith, that we will; and I will tell your worship more of the wart the next time we have confidence, and of other wooers.

Fenton. Well, farewell, I am in great haste now.

Quickly. Farewell to your worship. (*exit Fenton.*) Truly, an honest gentleman: but Anne loves him not; for I know Anne's mind as well as another does.—Out upon 't! what have I forgot?   *Exit*

The Merry We

f Windsor Act II

Scene I

Before Page's house

Enter Mistress Page, with a letter

Mrs. Page. What, have I scap'd love-letters in the holiday-time of my beauty, and am I now a subject for them? Let me see. *Reads*

'Ask me no reason why I love you, for though Love use Reason for his precisian, he admits him not for his counsellor: you are not young, no more am I; go to then, there's sympathy: you are merry, so am I; ha, ha! then there's more sympathy: you love sack, and so do I; would you desire better sympathy? Let it suffice thee, Mistress Page,—at the least if the love of soldier can suffice,—that I love thee: I will not say, pity me,—'tis not a soldier-like phrase; but I say, love me. By me,

> Thine own true knight,
> By day or night:
> Or any kind of light,
> With all his might,
> For thee to fight.—JOHN FALSTAFF.'

What a Herod of Jewry is this! O wicked, wicked world! One that is well-nigh worn to pieces with age to show himself a young gallant! What an unweigh'd behaviour hath this Flemish drunkard pick'd—with the devil's name! —out of my conversation, that he dares in this manner assay me? Why, he hath not been thrice in my company! What should I say to him? I was then frugal of my mirth: Heaven forgive me! Why, I'll exhibit a bill in the parliament for the putting down of men. How shall I be reveng'd on him? for reveng'd I will be, as sure as his guts are made of puddings.

Enter Mistress Ford

Mrs. Ford. Mistress Page, trust me, I was going to your house.

Mrs. Page. And trust me, I was coming to you: you look very ill.

Mrs. Ford. Nay, I'll ne'er believe that; I have to show to the contrary.

Mrs. Page. Faith, but you do, in my mind.

Mrs. Ford. Well, I do then; yet, I say, I could show you to the contrary. O Mistress Page, give me some counsel!

Mrs. Page. What's the matter, woman?

Mrs. Ford. O woman, if it were not for one trifling respect, I could come to such honour!

Mrs. Page. Hang the trifle, woman, take the honour. What is it?—dispense with trifles;—what is it?

Mrs. Ford. If I would but go to hell for an eternal moment or so, I could be knighted.

Mrs. Page. What? thou liest! Sir Alice Ford? These knights will hack, and so thou shouldst not alter the article of thy gentry.

Mrs. Ford. We burn daylight:—here, read, read; perceive how I might be knighted, I shall think the worse of fat men, as long as I have an eye to make difference of men's liking: and yet he would not swear; prais'd women's modesty; and gave such orderly and well-behav'd reproof to all uncomeliness, that I would have sworn his disposition would have gone to the truth of his words; but they do no more adhere and keep place together than the Hundredth Psalm to the tune of 'Green Sleeves.' What tempest, I trow, threw this whale (with so many tuns of oil in his belly) ashore at Windsor? How shall I be reveng'd on him? I think the best way were to entertain him with hope, till the wicked fire of lust have melted him in his own grease. Did you ever hear the like?

Mrs. Page. Letter for letter, but that the name of Page and Ford differs: to thy great comfort in this mystery of ill opinions, here's the twin-brother of thy letter: but let thine inherit first, for I protest mine never shall. I warrant he hath a thousand of these letters, writ with blank space for different names,—sure, more,—and these are of the second edition: he will print them, out of doubt; for he cares not what he puts into the press, when he would put us two. I had rather be a giantess, and lie under Mount Pelion. Well; I will find you twenty lascivious turtles ere one chaste man.

Mrs. Ford. Why, this is the very same; the very hand; the very words. What doth he think of us?

Mrs. Page. Nay, I know not: it makes me almost ready to wrangle with mine own honesty. I'll entertain myself like one that I am not acquainted withal; for, sure, unless he know some strain in me, that I know not myself, he would never have boarded me in this fury.

Mrs. Ford. 'Boarding,' call you it? I'll be sure to keep him above deck.

Mrs. Page. So will I: if he come under my hatches, I'll never to sea again. Let's be reveng'd on him: let's appoint him a meeting; give him a show of comfort in his suit, and lead him on with a fine-baited delay, till he hath pawn'd his horses to mine host of the Garter.

Mrs. Ford. Nay, I will consent to act any villany against him, that may not sully the chariness of our honesty. O, that my husband saw this letter! it would give eternal food to his jealousy.

Mrs. Page. Why, look where he comes; and my good man too: he's as far from jealousy as I am from giving him cause; and that, I hope, is an unmeasurable distance.

Mrs. Ford. You are the happier woman.

Mrs. Page. Let's consult together against this greasy knight. Come hither.   *They retire*

Enter Ford, with Pistol, and Page, with Nym

Ford. Well, I hope it be not so.

Pistol. Hope is a curtal dog in some affairs:
Sir John affects thy wife.

Ford. Why, sir, my wife is not young.

Pistol. He woos both high and low, both rich and poor,
Both young and old, one with another, Ford;
He loves the gallimaufry: Ford, perpend.

Ford. Love my wife?

Pistol. With liver burning hot. Prevent, or go thou,
Like Sir Actæon he, with Ringwood at thy heels:
O, odious is the name!

Ford. What name, sir?

Pistol. The horn, I say. Farewell.
Take heed, have open eye, for thieves do foot by night:
Take heed, ere summer comes, or cuckoo-birds do sing.

Away sir; Corporal Nym!—
Believe it, Page, he speaks sense.   *Exit*

Ford. (*aside*) I will be patient: I will find out this.

Nym. (*to Page*) And this is true; I like not the humour
of lying. He hath wronged me in some humours: I should
have borne the humour'd letter to her; but I have a sword,
and it shall bite upon my necessity. He loves your wife;
there's the short and the long. My name is Corporal Nym;
I speak, and I avouch; 'tis true: my name is Nym; and Falstaff loves your wife. Adieu. I love not the humour of
bread and cheese; [and there's the humour of it.] Adieu.
          Exit

Page. 'The humour of it,' quoth 'a? here's a fellow frights
English out of his wits.

Ford. I will seek out Falstaff.

Page. I never heard such a drawling, affecting rogue.

Ford. If I do find it:—well.

Page. I will not believe such a Cataian, though the priest
o' the town commended him for a true man.

Ford. 'Twas a good sensible fellow:—well.

Page. How now, Meg!

> *Mrs. Page and Mrs. Ford come forward*

Mrs. Page. Whither go you, George? Hark you.

Mrs. Ford. How now, sweet Frank, why art thou melancholy?

Ford. I melancholy? I am not melancholy. Get you home, go.

Mrs. Ford. Faith, thou hast some crotchets in thy head, now: will you go, Mistress Page?

Mrs. Page. Have with you. You'll come to dinner, George? (*aside to Mrs. Ford*) Look who comes yonder: she shall be our messenger to this paltry knight.

Mrs. Ford. (*aside to Mrs. Page*) Trust me, I thought on her: she'll fit it.

Enter Mistress Quickly

Mrs. Page. You are come to see my daughter Anne?

Quickly. Ay, forsooth; and, I pray, how does good Mistress Anne?

Mrs. Page. Go in with us and see: we have an hour's talk with you.

> *Exeunt Mrs. Page, Mrs. Ford, and Mrs. Quickly*

Page. How now, Master Ford?

Ford. You heard what this knave told me, did you not?

Page. Yes, and you heard what the other told me?

Ford. Do you think there is truth in them?

Page. Hang 'em, slaves! I do not think the knight would offer it: but these that accuse him in his intent towards our wives are a yoke of his discarded men; very rogues, now they be out of service.

Ford. Were they his men?

Page. Marry were they.

Ford. I like it never the better for that. Does he lie at the Garter?

Page. Ay marry does he. If he should intend this voyage towards my wife, I would turn her loose to him; and what he gets more of her than sharp words, let it lie on my head.

Ford. I do not misdoubt my wife; but I would be loath to turn them together: a man may be too confident: I would have nothing lie on my head: I cannot be thus satisfied.

Page. Look where my ranting host of the Garter comes: there is either liquor in his pate, or money in his purse, when he looks so merrily.

Enter Host

How now, mine host?

Host. How now, bully-rook! thou 'rt a gentleman. Cavaleiro-justice, I say!

Enter Shallow

Shallow. I follow, mine host, I follow. Good even, and twenty, good Master Page! Master Page, will you go with us? we have sport in hand.

Host. Tell him, cavaleiro-justice; tell him, bully-rook.

Shallow. Sir, there is a fray to be fought, between Sir Hugh the Welsh priest, and Caius the French doctor.

Ford. Good mine host o' the Garter, a word with you.

Drawing him aside

Host. What say'st thou, my bully-rook?

Shallow. (*to Page*) Will you go with us to behold it? My merry host hath had the measuring of their weapons; and, I think, hath appointed them contrary places; for, believe me, I hear the parson is no jester. Hark, I will tell you what our sport shall be.   *They converse apart*

Host. Hast thou no suit against my knight, my guest-cavaleire?

Ford. None, I protest: but I'll give you a pottle of burnt sack to give me recourse to him, and tell him my name is Brook; only for a jest.

Host. My hand, bully; thou shalt have egress and regress, (said I well?) and thy name shall be Brook. It is a merry knight. Will you go, An-heires?

Shallow. Have with you, mine host.

Page. I have heard the Frenchman hath good skill in his rapier.

Shallow. Tut, sir, I could have told you more. In these times you stand on distance; your passes, stoccadoes, and I know not what: 'tis the heart, Master Page, 'tis here, 'tis here: I have seen the time, with my long sword, I would have made you four tall fellows skip like rats.

Host. Here, boys, here, here! shall we wag?

Page. Have with you: I had rather hear them scold than fight.   *Exeunt Host, Shallow, and Page*

Ford. Though Page be a secure fool, and stands so firmly on his wife's frailty, yet I cannot put off my opinion so easily: she was in his company at Page's house; and what they made there, I know not. Well, I will look further into 't, and I have a disguise, to sound Falstaff; if I find her honest, I lose not my labour; if she be otherwise, 'tis labour well bestow'd.   *Exit*

Scene II

A room in the Garter Inn

Enter Falstaff and Pistol

[*Pistol*. I will retort the sum in equipage.]

Falstaff. I will not lend thee a penny.

Pistol. Why then the world's mine oyster,
Which I with sword will open.

Falstaff. Not a penny. I have been content, sir, you should lay my countenance to pawn: I have grated upon my good friends for three reprieves for you, and your coach-fellow Nym; or else you had looked through the grate, like a geminy of baboons. I am damn'd in hell, for swearing to gentlemen my friends, you were good soldiers, and tall fellows; and when Mistress Bridget lost the handle of her fan, I took 't upon mine honour thou hadst it not.

Pistol. Didst not thou share? hadst thou not fifteen pence?

Falstaff. Reason, you rogue, reason: think'st thou I'll endanger my soul gratis? At a word, hang no more about me, I am no gibbet for you. Go—a short knife and a throng!— to your manor of Pickt-hatch! Go; you'll not bear a letter for me, you rogue? you stand upon your honour? Why, thou unconfinable baseness, it is as much as I can do to keep the terms of my honour precise: I, I, I myself sometimes, leaving the fear of God on the left hand, and hiding mine honour in my necessity, am fain to shuffle, to hedge, and to lurch; and yet you, you rogue, will ensconce your rags, your cat-a-mountain looks, your red-lattice phrases, and your bold-beating oaths, under the shelter of your honour! You will not do it? you?

Pistol. I do relent: what would thou more of man?

Enter Robin

Robin. Sir, here's a woman would speak with you.
Falstaff. Let her approach.

Enter Mistress Quickly

Quickly. Give your worship good morrow.
Falstaff. Good morrow, good wife.
Quickly. Not so, an 't please your worship.
Falstaff. Good maid, then.
Quickly. I'll be sworn,
As my mother was, the first hour I was born.
Falstaff. I do believe the swearer. What with me?
Quickly. Shall I vouchsafe your worship a word or two?
Falstaff. Two thousand, fair woman: an I'll vouchsafe thee the hearing.
Quickly. There is one Mistress Ford, sir:—I pray, come a little nearer this ways:—I myself dwell with Master Doctor Caius,—
Falstaff. Well, on: Mistress Ford, you say,—
Quickly. Your worship says very true:—I pray your worship, come a little nearer this ways.
Falstaff. I warrant thee, nobody hears;—mine own people, mine own people.
Quickly. Are they so? God bless them, and make them his servants!
Falstaff. Well; Mistress Ford, what of her?
Quickly. Why, sir, she's a good creature.—Lord, Lord! your worship's a wanton! Well, heaven forgive you, and all of us, I pray!
Falstaff. Mistress Ford;—come, Mistress Ford,—
Quickly. Marry, this is the short and the long of it; you have brought her into such a canaries, as 'tis wonderful.

The best courtier of them all, when the court lay at Windsor, could never have brought her to such a canary. Yet there has been knights, and lords, and gentlemen, with their coaches; I warrant you, coach after coach, letter after letter, gift after gift, smelling so sweetly; all musk, and so rushling, I warrant you, in silk and gold, and in such alligant terms, and in such wine and sugar of the best, and the fairest, that would have won any woman's heart; and, I warrant you, they could never get an eye-wink of her: I had myself twenty angels given me this morning, but I defy all angels (in any such sort, as they say) but in the way of honesty: and, I warrant you, they could never get her so much as sip on a cup with the proudest of them all, and yet there has been earls; nay (which is more) pensioners; but, I warrant you, all is one with her.

Falstaff. But what says she to me? be brief, my good she-Mercury.

Quickly. Marry, she hath receiv'd your letter; for the which she thanks you a thousand times; and she gives you to notify, that her husband will be absence from his house, between ten and eleven.

Falstaff. Ten, and eleven.

Quickly. Ay, forsooth; and then you may come and see the picture, she says, that you wot of: Master Ford, her husband, will be from home. Alas, the sweet woman leads an ill life with him! he's a very jealousy man: she leads a very frampold life with him, good heart.

Falstaff. Ten, and eleven. Woman, commend me to her, I will not fail her.

Quickly. Why, you say well. But I have another messenger to your worship. Mistress Page hath her hearty commendations to you too: and let me tell you in your ear, she's as fartuous a civil modest wife, and one, I tell you, that will not miss you morning nor evening prayer, as any is in Windsor, whoe'er be the other: and she bade me tell your worship that her husband is seldom from home; but she

hopes there will come a time. I never knew a woman so
dote upon a man: surely, I think you have charms, la; yes,
in truth.

Falstaff. Not I, I assure thee: setting the attraction of my
good parts aside, I have no other charms.

Quickly. Blessing on your heart for 't!

Falstaff. But I pray thee tell me this: has Ford's wife and
Page's wife acquainted each other how they love me?

Quickly. That were a jest indeed! they have not so little
grace, I hope: that were a trick indeed! But Mistress Page
would desire you to send her your little page, of all loves:
her husband has a marvellous infection to the little page;
and, truly, Master Page is an honest man. Never a wife in
Windsor leads a better life than she does: do what she
will, say what she will, take all, pay all, go to bed when
she list, rise when she list, all is as she will: and truly she
deserves it; for if there be a kind woman in Windsor, she
is one. You must send her your page, no remedy.

Falstaff. Why, I will.

Quickly. Nay, but do so, then, and look you, he may come
and go between you both; and in any case have a nay-
word, that you may know one another's mind, and the boy
never need to understand any thing; for 'tis not good that
children should know any wickedness: old folks, you
know, have discretion, as they say, and know the world.

Falstaff. Fare thee well, commend me to them both: there's
my purse, I am yet thy debtor. Boy, go along with this
woman. (*exeunt Mistress Quickly and Robin.*) This news
distracts me!

Pistol. This punk is one of Cupid's carriers:
Clap on more sails, pursue; up with your fights:
Give fire: she is my prize, or ocean whelm them all!   *Exit*

Falstaff. Say'st thou so? Old Jack, go thy ways; I'll make
more of thy old body than I have done. Will they yet
look after thee? Wilt thou, after the expense of so much

money, be now a gainer? Good body, I thank thee. Let them say 'tis grossly done, so it be fairly done, no matter.

Enter Bardolph

Bardolph. Sir John, there's one Master Brook below would fain speak with you, and be acquainted with you; and hath sent your worship a morning's draught of sack.

Falstaff. Brook is his name?

Bardolph. Ay, sir.

Falstaff. Call him in. (*exit Bardolph.*) Such Brooks are welcome to me, that o'erflows such liquor. Ah, ha! Mistress Ford and Mistress Page, have I encompass'd you? go to; *via!*

Re-enter Bardolph, with Ford disguised

Ford. Bless you, sir!

Falstaff. And you, sir! Would you speak with me?

Ford. I make bold, to press with so little preparation upon you.

Falstaff. You're welcome. What's your will?—Give us leave, drawer.   *Exit Bardolph*

Ford. Sir, I am a gentleman that have spent much; my name is Brook.

Falstaff. Good Master Brook, I desire more acquaintance of you.

Ford. Good Sir John, I sue for yours: not to charge you; for I must let you understand I think myself in better plight for a lender than you are: the which hath something embolden'd me to this unseason'd intrusion; for they say, if money go before, all ways do lie open.

Falstaff. Money is a good soldier, sir, and will on.

Ford. Troth, and I have a bag of money here troubles me: if you will help to bear it, Sir John, take all, or half, for easing me of the carriage.

Falstaff. Sir, I know not how I may deserve to be your porter.

Ford. I will tell you, sir, if you will give me the hearing.

Falstaff. Speak, good Master Brook: I shall be glad to be your servant.

Ford. Sir, I hear you are a scholar, (I will be brief with you) and you have been a man long known to me, though I had never so good means, as desire, to make myself acquainted with you. I shall discover a thing to you, wherein I must very much lay open mine own imperfection: but, good Sir John, as you have one eye upon my follies, as you hear them unfolded, turn another into the register of your own, that I may pass with a reproof the easier, sith you yourself know how easy it is to be such an offender.

Falstaff. Very well, sir; proceed.

Ford. There is a gentlewoman in this town, her husband's name is Ford.

Falstaff. Well, sir.

Ford. I have long lov'd her, and, I protest to you, bestowed much on her; followed her with a doting observance; engross'd opportunities to meet her; fee'd every slight occasion that could but niggardly give me sight of her; not only bought many presents to give her, but have given largely to many, to know what she would have given; briefly, I have pursued her, as love hath pursued me, which hath been on the wing of all occasions. But whatsoever I have merited, either in my mind, or in my means, meed I am sure I have received none, unless experience be a jewel that I have purchased at an infinite rate, and that hath taught me to say this:

'Love like a shadow flies, when substance love pursues,
Pursuing that that flies, and flying what pursues.'

Falstaff. Have you receiv'd no promise of satisfaction at her hands?

Ford. Never.

Falstaff. Have you importun'd her to such a purpose?

Ford. Never.

Falstaff. Of what quality was your love, then?

Ford. Like a fair house, built on another man's ground, so that I have lost my edifice, by mistaking the place where I erected it.

Falstaff. To what purpose have you unfolded this to me?

Ford. When I have told you that, I have told you all. Some say, that though she appear honest to me, yet in other places she enlargeth her mirth so far that there is shrewd construction made of her. Now, Sir John, here is the heart of my purpose: you are a gentleman of excellent breeding, admirable discourse, of great admittance, authentic in your place and person, generally allow'd for your many war-like, court-like, and learned preparations.

Falstaff. O, sir!

Ford. Believe it, for you know it. There is money; spend it, spend it, spend more; spend all I have, only give me so much of your time in exchange of it, as to lay an amiable siege to the honesty of this Ford's wife: use your art of wooing; win her to consent to you: if any man may, you may as soon as any.

Falstaff. Would it apply well to the vehemency of your affection, that I should win what you would enjoy? Methinks you prescribe to yourself very preposterously.

Ford. O, understand my drift. She dwells so securely on the excellency of her honour, that the folly of my soul dares not present itself: she is too bright to be look'd against. Now, could I come to her with any detection in my hand, my desires had instance and argument to commend themselves: I could drive her then from the ward of her purity, her reputation, her marriage-vow, and a thousand other her defences, which now are too too strongly embattled against me. What say you to 't, Sir John?

Falstaff. Master Brook, I will first make bold with your money; next, give me your hand; and last, as I am a gentleman, you shall, if you will, enjoy Ford's wife.

Ford. O good sir!

Falstaff. I say you shall.

Ford. Want no money, Sir John, you shall want none.

Falstaff. Want no Mistress Ford, Master Brook, you shall want none. I shall be with her (I may tell you) by her own appointment; even as you came in to me, her assistant, or go-between, parted from me: I say I shall be with her between ten and eleven; for at that time the jealous rascally knave her husband will be forth. Come you to me at night, you shall know how I speed.

Ford. I am blest in your acquaintance. Do you know Ford, sir?

Falstaff. Hang him, poor cuckoldly knave, I know him not: yet I wrong him to call him poor; they say the jealous wittolly knave hath masses of money, for the which his wife seems to me well-favour'd: I will use her as the key of the cuckoldly rogue's coffer, and there's my harvest-home.

Ford. I would you knew Ford, sir, that you might avoid him, if you saw him.

Falstaff. Hang him, mechanical salt-butter rogue; I will stare him out of his wits; I will awe him with my cudgel: it shall hang like a meteor o'er the cuckold's horns. Master Brook, thou shalt know I will predominate over the peasant, and thou shalt lie with his wife. Come to me soon at night. Ford's a knave, and I will aggravate his style; thou, Master Brook, shalt know him for knave, and cuckold. Come to me soon at night.   *Exit*

Ford. What a damn'd Epicurean rascal is this! My heart is ready to crack with impatience. Who says this is improvident jealousy? my wife hath sent to him, the hour is fix'd, the match is made: would any man have thought this? See the hell of having a false woman! My bed shall be abus'd, my coffers ransack'd, my reputation gnawn at, and I shall not only receive this villanous wrong, but stand under the adoption of abominable terms, and by him that does me this wrong. Terms! names!—Amaimon sounds well; Lucifer, well; Barbason, well; yet they are devils' additions, the names of fiends: but Cuckold, Wittol, Cuckold? the devil himself hath not such a name. Page is an ass, a secure ass: he will trust his wife; he will not be jealous. I will rather trust a Fleming with my butter, Parson Hugh the Welshman with my cheese, an Irishman with my aqua-vitæ bottle, or a thief to walk my ambling gelding, than my wife with herself: then she plots, then she ruminates, then she devises; and what they think in their hearts they may effect, they will break their hearts but they will effect. God be prais'd for my jealousy!—Eleven o'clock the hour. I will prevent this, detect my wife, be reveng'd on Falstaff, and laugh at Page. I will about it, better three hours too soon, than a minute too late. Fie, fie, fie! cuckold! cuckold! cuckold!   *Exit*

Scene III

A field near Windsor

Enter Caius and Rugby

Caius. Jack Rugby!

Rugby. Sir?

Caius. Vat is de clock, Jack?

Rugby. 'Tis past the hour, sir, that Sir Hugh promis'd to meet.

Caius. By gar, he has save his soul, dat he is no-come; he has pray his Pible well, dat he is no-come: by gar, Jack Rugby, he is dead already, if he be come.

Rugby. He is wise, sir; he knew your worship would kill him if he came.

Caius. By gar, de herring is no dead, so as I vill kill him. Take your rapier, Jack, I vill tell you how I vill kill him.

Rugby. Alas, sir, I cannot fence.

Caius. Villainy, take your rapier.

Rugby. Forbear; here's company.

Enter Host, Shallow, Slender, and Page

Host. Bless thee, bully doctor!

Shallow. Save you, Master Doctor Caius!

Page. Now, good master doctor!

Slender. Give you good morrow, sir.

Caius. Vat be all you, one, two, tree, four, come for?

Host. To see thee fight, to see thee foin, to see thee traverse, to see thee here, to see thee there, to see thee pass thy punto, thy stock, thy reverse, thy distance, thy montant. Is he dead, my Ethiopian? is he dead, my Francisco? ha, bully! What says my Æsculapius? my Galen? my heart of elder? ha! is he dead, bully-stale? is he dead?

Caius. By gar, he is de coward Jack priest of de vorld; he is not show his face.

Host. Thou art a Castalion-King-Urinal. Hector of Greece, my boy!

Caius. I pray you, bear vitness that me have stay, six or seven, two tree hours for him, and he is no-come.

Shallow. He is the wiser man, master doctor: he is a curer of souls, and you a curer of bodies; if you should fight, you go against the hair of your professions. Is it not true, Master Page?

Page. Master Shallow, you have yourself been a great fighter, though now a man of peace.

Shallow. Bodykins, Master Page, though I now be old, and of the peace, if I see a sword out, my finger itches to make one. Though we are justices, and doctors, and churchmen, Master Page, we have some salt of our youth in us, we are the sons of women, Master Page.

Page. 'Tis true, Master Shallow.

Shallow. It will be found so, Master Page. Master Doctor Caius, I am come to fetch you home. I am sworn of the peace: you have shew'd yourself a wise physician, and Sir Hugh hath shewn himself a wise and patient churchman. You must go with me, master doctor.

Host. Pardon, guest-justice.—A [word,] Mounseur Mock-water.

Caius. Mock-vater? vat is dat?

Host. Mock-water, in our English tongue, is valour, bully.

Caius. By gar, den, I have as much mock-vater as de Eng-lishman.—Scurvy Jack-dog priest! by gar, me vill cut his ears.

Host. He will clapper-claw thee tightly, bully.

Caius. Clapper-de-claw? vat is dat?

Host. That is, he will make thee amends.

Caius. By gar, me do look he shall clapper-de-claw me; for, by gar, me vill have it.

Host. And I will provoke him to 't, or let him wag.

Caius. Me tank you for dat.

Host. And, moreover, bully,—But first, master guest, and Master Page, and eke Cavaleiro Slender, go you through the town to Frogmore.   *Aside to them*

Page. Sir Hugh is there, is he?

Host. He is there: see what humour he is in; and I will bring the doctor about by the fields. Will it do well?

Shallow. We will do it.

Page, Shallow, and Slender. Adieu, good master doctor.
                          Exeunt Page, Shallow, and Slender

Caius. By gar, me vill kill de priest, for he speak for a jack-an-ape to Anne Page.

Host. Let him die: sheathe thy impatience; throw cold water on thy choler: go about the fields with me through Frogmore, I will bring thee where Mistress Anne Page is, at a farm-house a-feasting; and thou shalt woo her. Cried-game, said I well?

Caius. By gar, me dank you vor dat: by gar, I love you; and I shall procure-a you de good guest; de earl, de knight, de lords, de gentlemen, my patients.

Host. For the which, I will be thy adversary toward Anne Page. Said I well?

Caius. By gar, 'tis good; vell said.

Host. Let us wag, then.

Caius. Come at my heels, Jack Rugby.   *Exeunt*

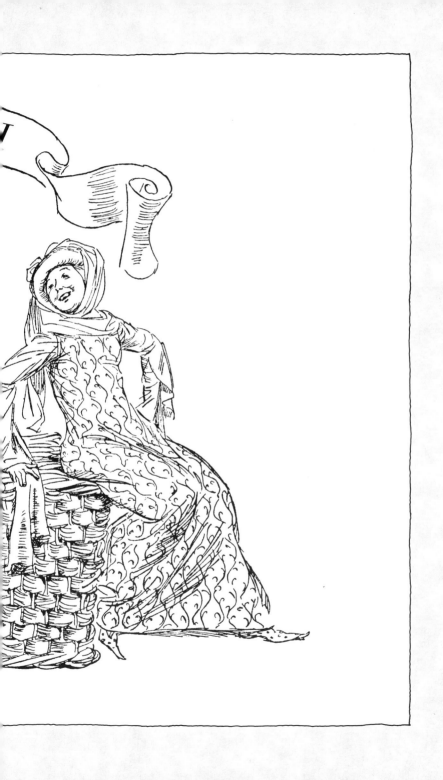

Scene I

A field near Frogmore

Enter Sir Hugh Evans and Simple

Evans. I pray you now, good Master Slender's serving-man,
and friend Simple by your name, which way have you
look'd for Master Caius, that calls himself doctor of
physic?

Simple. Marry, sir, the pittie-ward, the park-ward, every
way; old Windsor way, and every way but the town way.

Evans. I most fehemently desire you you will also look that
way.

Simple. I will, sir.   *Exit*

Evans. Jeshu pless me! how full of chollors I am, and trem-
pling of mind; I shall be glad if he have deceiv'd me; how
melancholies I am!—I will knog his urinals about his
knave's costard when I have goot opportunities for the
'ork.—Pless my soul!—   *Sings*

> To shallow rivers, to whose falls
> Melodious birds sings madrigals;
> There will we make our peds of roses,
> And a thousand fragrant posies.
> To shallow—

Now, so Kad 'udge me, I have a great dispositions to cry.
                                                    Sings

> Melodious birds sing madrigals—
> Whenas I sat in Pabylon—

And a thousand vagram posies.
To shallow etc.

Re-enter Simple

Simple. Yonder he is coming, this way, Sir Hugh.
Evans. He's welcome.—   *Sings*
          To shallow rivers, to whose falls—
Heaven prosper the right!—What weapon is he?
Simple. No weapons, sir. There comes my master, Master
          Shallow, and another gentleman; from Frogmore, over
          the stile, this way.
Evans. Pray you give me my gown, or else keep it in your
          arms.

Enter Page, Shallow, and Slender

Shallow. How now, master parson? Good morrow, good Sir
          Hugh. Keep a gamester from the dice, and a good student
          from his book, and it is wonderful.
Slender. (*aside*) Ah, sweet Anne Page!
Page. God save you, good Sir Hugh!
Evans. Got pless you from his mercy sake, all of you!
Shallow. What, the sword, and the word? do you study
          them both, master parson?
Page. And youthful still, in your doublet and hose, this raw
          rheumatic day!
Evans. There is reasons, and causes for it.
Page. We are come to you, to do a good office, master
          parson.
Evans. Fery well: what is it?
Page. Yonder is a most reverend gentleman; who, belike,
          having receiv'd wrong by some person, is at most odds
          with his own gravity and patience that ever you saw.
Shallow. I have lived fourscore years, and upward; I never
          heard a man of his place, gravity, and learning, so wide of
          his own respect.
Evans. What is he?

Page. I think you know him; Master Doctor Caius, the re-
nown'd French physician.

Evans. Got's will, and his passion of my heart! I had as lief
you would tell me of a mess of porridge.

Page. Why?

Evans. He has no more knowledge in Hibocrates and
Galen, and he is a knave besides; a cowardly knave as
you would desires to be acquainted withal.

Page. I warrant you, he's the man should fight with him.

Slender. (*aside*) O sweet Anne Page!

Shallow. It appears so by his weapons: keep them asunder:
here comes Doctor Caius.

Enter Host, Caius, and Rugby

Page. Nay, good master parson, keep in your weapon.

Shallow. So do you, good master doctor.

Host. Disarm them, and let them question: let them keep
their limbs whole, and hack our English.

Caius. I pray you let-a me speak a word with your ear. Vere-
fore vill you not meet-a me?

Evans. (*aside to Caius*) Pray you, use your patience: in
good time.

Caius. By gar, you are de coward; de Jack dog; John Ape.

Evans. (*aside to Caius*) Pray you let us not be laughing-
stocks to other men's humours; I desire you in friendship,
and I will one way or other make you amends. (*aloud*)
Py Jeshu, I will knog your urinal about your knave's cogs-
comb [for missing your meetings and appointments].

Caius. Diable!—Jack Rugby,—mine host de Jarteer,—have I
not stay for him, to kill him? have I not at de place I did
appoint?

Evans. As I am a Christians soul, now look you; this is the
place appointed: I'll be judgement by mine host of the
Garter.

Host. Peace, I say, Gallia and Gaul, French and Welsh,
soul-curer and body-curer!

Caius. Ay, dat is very good, excellent.

Host. Peace, I say! hear mine host of the Garter. Am I politic? am I subtle? am I a Machiavel? Shall I lose my doctor? no, he gives me the potions and the motions. Shall I lose my parson? my priest? my Sir Hugh? no, he gives me the proverbs, and the no-verbs. [Give me thy hand, terrestrial; so.] Give me thy hand, celestial; so. Boys of art, I have deceiv'd you both; I have directed you to wrong places; your hearts are mighty, your skins are whole, and let burnt sack be the issue. Come, lay their swords to pawn. Follow me, lads of peace; follow, follow, follow.

Shallow. Afore God, a mad host. Follow, gentlemen, follow.

Slender. (*aside*) O sweet Anne Page!

Exeunt Shallow, Slender, Page, and Host

Caius. Ha, do I perceive dat? have you make-a de sot of us, ha, ha?

Evans. This is well, he has made us his vlouting-stog: I desire you that we may be friends; and let us knog our prains together to be revenge on this same scall, scurvy, cogging companion, the host of the Garter.

Caius. By gar, with all my heart. He promise to bring me where is Anne Page; by gar, he deceive me too.

Evans. Well, I will smite his noddles: pray you follow.

Exeunt

Scene II

Enter Mistress Page and Robin

Mrs. Page. Nay, keep your way, little gallant; you were wont to be a follower, but now you are a leader. Whether had you rather lead mine eyes, or eye your master's heels?

Robin. I had rather, forsooth, go before you like a man, than follow him like a dwarf.

Mrs. Page. O, you are a flattering boy, now I see you'll be a courtier.

Enter Ford

Ford. Well met, Mistress Page, whither go you?

Mrs. Page. Truly, sir, to see your wife; is she at home?

Ford. Ay, and as idle as she may hang together, for want of company. I think, if your husbands were dead, you two would marry.

Mrs. Page. Be sure of that,—two other husbands.

Ford. Where had you this pretty weathercock?

Mrs. Page. I cannot tell what the dickens his name is my husband had him of.—What do you call your knight's name, sirrah?

Robin. Sir John Falstaff.

Ford. Sir John Falstaff?

Mrs. Page. He, he, I can never hit on 's name. There is such a league between my good man and he!—Is your wife at home indeed?

Ford. Indeed she is.

Mrs. Page. By your leave, sir, I am sick till I see her.

Exeunt Mrs. Page and Robin

Ford. Has Page any brains? hath he any eyes? hath he any thinking? Sure they sleep, he hath no use of them. Why, this boy will carry a letter twenty mile, as easy as a cannon will shoot point-blank twelve score. He pieces out his wife's inclination; he gives her folly motion and advantage: and now she's going to my wife, and Falstaff's boy with her. A man may hear this shower sing in the wind. And Falstaff's boy with her! Good plots, they are laid, and our revolted wives share damnation together. Well, I will take him, then torture my wife, pluck the borrow'd veil of modesty from the so-seeming Mistress Page, divulge Page himself for a secure and wilful Actæon, and to these violent proceedings all my neighbours shall cry aim. (*Clock heard.*) The clock gives me my cue, and my assurance bids me search, there I shall find Falstaff: I shall be rather prais'd for this than mock'd, for it is as positive as the earth is firm that Falstaff is there: I will go.

Enter Page, Shallow, Slender, Host, Sir Hugh Evans,
Caius, and Rugby

Shallow, Page, &c. Well met, Master Ford.

Ford. Trust me, a good knot: I have good cheer at home, and I pray you all go with me.

Shallow. I must excuse myself, Master Ford.

Slender. And so must I sir, we have appointed to dine with Mistress Anne, and I would not break with her for more money than I'll speak of.

Shallow. We have linger'd about a match between Anne Page and my cousin Slender, and this day we shall have our answer.

Slender. I hope I have your good will, father Page.

Page. You have, Master Slender, I stand wholly for you, but my wife, master doctor, is for you altogether.

Caius. Ay, be-gar, and de maid is love-a me: my nursh-a
Quickly tell me so mush.

Host. What say you to young Master Fenton? he capers, he
dances, he has eyes of youth; he writes verses, he speaks
holiday, he smells April and May, he will carry 't, he will
carry 't, 'tis in his buttons, he will carry 't.

Page. Not by my consent, I promise you. The gentleman is
of no having, he kept company with the wild prince and
Poins; he is of too high a region; he knows too much. No,
he shall not knit a knot in his fortunes with the finger of
my substance: if he take her, let him take her simply; the
wealth I have waits on my consent, and my consent goes
not that way.

Ford. I beseech you heartily, some of you go home with me
to dinner: besides your cheer, you shall have sport, I will
show you a monster. Master doctor, you shall go, so shall
you, Master Page, and you, Sir Hugh.

Shallow. Well, fare you well: we shall have the freer wooing at Master Page's.   *Exeunt Shallow and Slender*

Caius. Go home, John Rugby; I come anon.   *Exit Rugby*

Host. Farewell, my hearts, I will to my honest knight Falstaff, and drink canary with him.   *Exit*

Ford. (*aside*) I think I shall drink in pipe-wine first with
him, I'll make him dance. Will you go, gentles?

All. Have with you, to see this monster.   *Exeunt*

Scene III

A room in Ford's house

Enter Mistress Ford and Mistress Page

Mrs. Ford. What, John! What, Robert!

Mrs. Page. Quickly, quickly!—is the buck-basket—

Mrs. Ford. I warrant. What, Robin, I say!

Enter Servants with a great buck-basket

Mrs. Page. Come, come, come.

Mrs. Ford. Here, set it down.

Mrs. Page. Give your men the charge, we must be brief.

Mrs. Ford. Marry, as I told you before, John and Robert, be ready here hard by in the brew-house, and when I suddenly call you, come forth, and (without any pause, or staggering) take this basket on your shoulders: that done, trudge with it in all haste, and carry it among the whitsters in Datchet Mead, and there empty it in the muddy ditch, close by the Thames side.

Mrs. Page. You will do it?

Mrs. Ford. I ha' told them over and over, they lack no direction. Be gone, and come when you are call'd.

Exeunt Servants

Mrs. Page. Here comes little Robin.

Enter Robin

Mrs. Ford. How now, my eyas-musket, what news with you?

Robin. My master, Sir John, is come in at your back-door, Mistress Ford, and requests your company.

Mrs. Page. You little Jack-a-Lent, have you been true to us?

Robin. Ay, I'll be sworn. My master knows not of your being here; and hath threaten'd to put me into everlasting liberty, if I tell you of it; for he swears he'll turn me away.

Mrs. Page. Thou 'rt a good boy: this secrecy of thine shall be a tailor to thee, and shall make thee a new doublet and hose. I'll go hide me.

Mrs. Ford. Do so. Go tell thy master I am alone. (*exit Robin.*) Mistress Page, remember you your cue.

Mrs. Page. I warrant thee, if I do not act it, hiss me.   *Exit*

Mrs. Ford. Go to, then: we'll use this unwholesome humidity, this gross watery pumpion; we'll teach him to know turtles from jays.

Enter Falstaff

Falstaff. 'Have I caught' thee, 'my heavenly jewel?' Why, now let me die, for I have liv'd long enough: this is the period of my ambition: O this blessed hour!

Mrs. Ford. O sweet Sir John!

Falstaff. Mistress Ford, I cannot cog, I cannot prate, Mistress Ford; now shall I sin in my wish: I would thy husband were dead, I'll speak it before the best lord, I would make thee my lady.

Mrs. Ford. I your lady, Sir John? alas, I should be a pitiful lady!

Falstaff. Let the court of France show me such another. I see how thine eye would emulate the diamond: thou hast the right arched beauty of the brow, that becomes the ship-tire, the tire-valiant, or any tire of Venetian admittance.

Mrs. Ford. A plain kerchief, Sir John: my brows become nothing else, nor that well neither.

Falstaff. By the Lord, thou art a traitor to say so: thou wouldst make an absolute courtier, and the firm fixture of thy foot would give an excellent motion to thy gait, in a semicircled farthingale. I see what thou wert, if Fortune thy foe were not, Nature thy friend. Come, thou canst not hide it.

Mrs. Ford. Believe me, there's no such thing in me.

Falstaff. What made me love thee? Let that persuade thee: there's something extraordinary in thee: come, I cannot cog, and say thou art this and that, like a many of these lisping hawthorn-buds, that come like women in men's apparel, and smell like Bucklersbury in simple time; I cannot, but I love thee, none but thee; and thou deserv'st it.

Mrs. Ford. Do not betray me, sir, I fear you love Mistress Page.

Falstaff. Thou mightst as well say, I love to walk by the Counter-gate, which is as hateful to me as the reek of a lime-kiln.

Mrs. Ford. Well, heaven knows how I love you, and you shall one day find it.

Falstaff. Keep in that mind, I'll deserve it.

Mrs. Ford. Nay, I must tell you, so you do; or else I could not be in that mind.

Robin. (*within*) Mistress Ford, Mistress Ford! here's Mistress Page at the door, sweating, and blowing, and looking wildly, and would needs speak with you presently.

Falstaff. She shall not see me, I will ensconce me behind the arras.

Mrs. Ford. Pray you do so, she's a very tattling woman.

Falstaff hides himself

Re-enter Mistress Page and Robin

What's the matter? how now?

Mrs. Page. O Mistress Ford, what have you done? You're sham'd, you're overthrown, you're undone for ever!

Mrs. Ford. What's the matter, good Mistress Page?

Mrs. Page. O well-a-day, Mistress Ford! having an honest man to your husband, to give him such cause of suspicion!

Mrs. Ford. What cause of suspicion?

Mrs. Page. What cause of suspicion? Out upon you! how am I mistook in you!

Mrs. Ford. Why, alas, what's the matter?

Mrs. Page. Your husband's coming hither, woman, with all the officers in Windsor, to search for a gentleman, that he says is here now in the house; by your consent to take an ill advantage of his absence: you are undone.

Mrs. Ford. 'Tis not so, I hope.

Mrs. Page. Pray heaven it be not so, that you have such a man here! but 'tis most certain your husband's coming, with half Windsor at his heels, to search for such a one; I come before to tell you. If you know yourself clear, why, I am glad of it; but if you have a friend here, convey, convey him out. Be not amaz'd, call all your senses to you, defend your reputation, or bid farewell to your good life for ever.

Mrs. Ford. What shall I do? There is a gentleman my dear friend; and I fear not mine own shame so much, as his peril. I had rather than a thousand pound he were out of the house.

Mrs. Page. For shame! never stand; ('you had rather' and 'you had rather'!) your husband's here at hand; bethink you of some conveyance: in the house you cannot hide him. O, how have you deceiv'd me! Look, here is a basket, if he be of any reasonable stature, he may creep in here, and throw foul linen upon him, as if it were going to bucking: or,—it is whiting-time,—send him by your two men to Datchet Mead.

Mrs. Ford. He's too big to go in there. What shall I do?

Falstaff. (*coming forward*) Let me see 't, let me see 't, O, let

me see 't!—I'll in, I'll in.—Follow your friend's counsel.—
I'll in.

Mrs. Page. What, Sir John Falstaff? Are these your letters,
knight?

Falstaff. I love thee.—Help me away.—Let me creep in here.
—I'll never—

      Gets into the basket; they cover him with foul linen

Mrs. Page. Help to cover your master, boy.—Call your men,
Mistress Ford.—You dissembling knight!

Mrs. Ford. What, John! Robert! John!   *Exit Robin*

      Re-enter Servants

Go, take up these clothes here, quickly.—Where's the
cowl-staff? look how you drumble!—Carry them to the
laundress in Datchet Mead; quickly, come.

      Enter Ford, Page, Caius, and Sir Hugh Evans

Ford. Pray you come near: if I suspect without cause, why
then make sport at me, then let me be your jest, I deserve
it.—How now? whither bear you this?

Servant. To the laundress, forsooth.

Mrs. Ford. Why, what have you to do whither they bear it?
You were best meddle with buck-washing!

Ford. Buck?—I would I could wash myself of the buck!—
Buck, buck, buck, ay, buck; I warrant you, buck; and of
the season too; it shall appear. (*exeunt Servants with the
basket.*) Gentlemen, I have dream'd to-night, I'll tell you
my dream. Here, here, here be my keys, ascend my chambers, search, seek, find out: I'll warrant we'll unkennel the
fox. Let me stop this way first. (*Locking the door.*) So,
now uncape.

Page. Good Master Ford, be contented: you wrong yourself
too much.

Ford. True, Master Page. Up, gentlemen, you shall see sport
anon: follow me, gentlemen.   **Exit**

Evans. This is fery fantastical humours and jealousies.

Caius. By gar, 'tis no the fashion of France; it is not jealous
in France.

Page. Nay, follow him, gentlemen, see the issue of his search.

Exeunt Page, Caius, and Evans

Mrs. Page. Is there not a double excellency in this?

Mrs. Ford. I know not which pleases me better, that my
husband is deceiv'd, or Sir John.

Mrs. Page. What a taking was he in, when your husband
ask'd who was in the basket!

Mrs. Ford. I am half afraid he will have need of washing; so
throwing him into the water will do him a benefit.

Mrs. Page. Hang him, dishonest rascal! I would all of the
same strain were in the same distress.

Mrs. Ford. I think my husband hath some special suspicion
of Falstaff's being here; for I never saw him so gross in his
jealousy till now.

Mrs. Page. I will lay a plot to try that, and we will yet have
more tricks with Falstaff: his dissolute disease will scarce
obey this medicine.

Mrs. Ford. Shall we send that foolish carrion, Mistress
Quickly, to him, and excuse his throwing into the water,
and give him another hope, to betray him to another pun-
ishment?

Mrs. Page. We will do it: let him be sent for to-morrow
eight o'clock, to have amends.

Re-enter Ford, Page, Caius, and Sir Hugh Evans

Ford. I cannot find him: may be the knave bragg'd of that
he could not compass.

Mrs. Page. (*aside to Mrs. Ford*) Heard you that?

Mrs. Ford. You use me well, Master Ford, do you?

Ford. Ay, I do so.

Mrs. Ford. Heaven make you better than your thoughts!

Ford. Amen!

Mrs. Page. You do yourself mighty wrong, Master Ford.

Ford. Ay, ay; I must bear it.

Evans. By Jeshu, if there be any pody in the house, and in the chambers, and in the coffers, and in the presses, heaven forgive my sins at the day of judgement!

Caius. By gar, nor I too: there is no bodies.

Page. Fie, fie, Master Ford! are you not asham'd? What spirit, what devil suggests this imagination? I would not ha' your distemper in this kind for the wealth of Windsor Castle.

Ford. 'Tis my fault, Master Page: I suffer for it.

Evans. You suffer for a pad conscience: your wife is as honest a 'omans as I will desires among five thousand, and five hundred too.

Caius. By gar, I see 'tis an honest woman.

Ford. Well, I promis'd you a dinner. Come, come, walk in the park, I pray you pardon me; I will hereafter make known to you why I have done this. Come, wife, come, Mistress Page, I pray you pardon me; pray heartily pardon me.

Page. Let's go in, gentlemen, but, trust me, we'll mock him. I do invite you to-morrow morning to my house to breakfast: after, we'll a-birding together; I have a fine hawk for the bush. Shall it be so?

Ford. Any thing.

Evans. If there is one, I shall make two in the company.

Caius. If there be one, or two, I shall make-a the turd.

Ford. Pray you, go, Master Page.

Evans. I pray you now, remembrance to-morrow on the lousy knave, mine host.

Caius. Dat is good, by gar, with all my heart.

Evans. A lousy knave, to have his gibes, and his mockeries!

Exeunt

Scene IV

Enter Fenton and Anne Page

Fenton. I see I cannot get thy father's love;
   Therefore no more turn me to him, sweet Nan.
Anne. Alas, how then?
Fenton.   Why, thou must be thyself.
   He doth object, I am too great of birth,
   And that, my state being gall'd with my expense,
   I seek to heal it only by his wealth:
   Besides these, other bars he lays before me,
   My riots past, my wild societies,
   And tells me 'tis a thing impossible
   I should love thee, but as a property.
Anne. May be he tells you true.
Fenton. No, heaven so speed me in my time to come!
   Albeit I will confess, thy father's wealth
   Was the first motive that I woo'd thee, Anne:
   Yet, wooing thee, I found thee of more value
   Than stamps in gold, or sums in sealed bags;
   And 'tis the very riches of thyself
   That now I aim at.
Anne.   Gentle Master Fenton,
   Yet seek my father's love, still seek it, sir;
   If opportunity and humblest suit
   Cannot attain it, why, then,—hark you hither!

They converse apart

Enter Shallow, Slender, and Mistress Quickly

Shallow. Break their talk, Mistress Quickly: my kinsman shall speak for himself.
Slender. I'll make a shaft or a bolt on 't: 'slid, 'tis but venturing.

Shallow. Be not dismay'd.

Slender. No, she shall not dismay me: I care not for that, but that I am afeard.

Quickly. Hark ye, Master Slender would speak a word with you.

Anne. I come to him. (*aside*) This is my father's choice.
O, what a world of vile ill-favour'd faults
Looks handsome in three hundred pounds a-year!

Quickly. And how does good Master Fenton? Pray you, a word with you.

Shallow. She's coming; to her, coz. O boy, thou hadst a father!

Slender. I had a father, Mistress Anne, my uncle can tell you good jests of him. Pray you, uncle, tell Mistress Anne the jest how my father stole two geese out of a pen, good uncle.

Shallow. Mistress Anne, my cousin loves you.

Slender. Ay, that I do, as well as I love any woman in Gloucestershire.

Shallow. He will maintain you like a gentlewoman.

Slender. Ay, that I will, come cut and long-tail, under the degree of a squire.

Shallow. He will make you a hundred and fifty pounds join-ture.

Anne. Good Master Shallow, let him woo for himself.

Shallow. Marry, I thank you for it; I thank you for that good comfort. She calls you, coz, I'll leave you.

Anne. Now, Master Slender,—

Slender. Now, good Mistress Anne,—

Anne. What is your will?

Slender. My will? od's heartlings, that's a pretty jest indeed! I ne'er made my will yet, I thank heaven; I am not such a sickly creature, I give heaven praise.

Anne. I mean, Master Slender, what would you with me?

Slender. Truly, for mine own part, I would little or nothing with you: your father and my uncle hath made motions:

if it be my luck, so; if not, happy man be his dole! They
can tell you how things go, better than I can: you may ask
your father, here he comes.

Enter Page and Mistress Page

Page. Now, Master Slender: love him, daughter Anne.—
    Why, how now? what does Master Fenton here?
    You wrong me, sir, thus still to haunt my house:
    I told you, sir, my daughter is dispos'd of.
Fenton. Nay, Master Page, be not impatient.
Mrs. Page. Good Master Fenton, come not to my child.
Page. She is no match for you.
Fenton. Sir, will you hear me?
Page.   No, good Master Fenton.
    Come, Master Shallow; come, son Slender, in.
    Knowing my mind, you wrong me, Master Fenton.
            Exeunt Page, Shallow, and Slender
Quickly. Speak to Mistress Page.
Fenton. Good Mistress Page, for that I love your daughter
    In such a righteous fashion as I do,
    Perforce, against all checks, rebukes, and manners,
    I must advance the colours of my love,
    And not retire: let me have your good will.
Anne. Good mother, do not marry me to yond fool.
Mrs. Page. I mean it not, I seek you a better husband.
Quickly. That's my master, master doctor.
Anne. Alas, I had rather be set quick i' the earth,
    And bowl'd to death with turnips!
Mrs. Page. Come, trouble not yourself, good Master Fenton,
    I will not be your friend, nor enemy:
    My daughter will I question how she loves you,
    And as I find her, so am I affected.
    Till then, farewell, sir, she must needs go in,
    Her father will be angry.
Fenton. Farewell, gentle mistress: farewell, Nan.
            Exeunt Mrs. Page and Anne

Quickly. This is my doing now: 'Nay,' said I, 'will you cast
away your child on a fool, and a physician? Look on Master Fenton:' this is my doing.

Fenton. I thank thee; and I pray thee once to-night
Give my sweet Nan this ring: there's for thy pains.

Quickly. Now heaven send thee good fortune! (*exit Fenton.*) A kind heart he hath: a woman would run through
fire and water for such a kind heart. But yet I would my
master had Mistress Anne, or I would Master Slender had
her; or, in sooth, I would Master Fenton had her: I will
do what I can for them all three, for so I have promis'd,
and I'll be as good as my word, but speciously for Master
Fenton. Well, I must of another errand to Sir John Falstaff from my two mistresses: what a beast am I to slack
it!   *Exit*

Scene V

Falstaff. Bardolph, I say,—

Bardolph. Here, sir.

Falstaff. Go fetch me a quart of sack, put a toast in 't. (*exit Bardolph.*) Have I liv'd to be carried in a basket, like a barrow of butcher's offal? and to be thrown in the Thames? Well, if I be serv'd such another trick, I'll have my brains ta'en out and butter'd, and give them to a dog for a new-year's gift. The rogues slighted me into the river with as little remorse, as they would have drown'd a blind bitch's puppies, fifteen i' the litter: and you may know by my size, that I have a kind of alacrity in sinking; if the bottom were as deep as hell, I should down. I had been drown'd, but that the shore was shelvy and shallow; a death that I abhor; for the water swells a man; and what a thing should I have been, when I had been swell'd! I should have been a mountain of mummy.

Re-enter Bardolph with sack

Bardolph. Here's Mistress Quickly, sir, to speak with you.

Falstaff. Come, let me pour in some sack to the Thames water; for my belly's as cold as if I had swallow'd snow-balls, for pills to cool the reins. Call her in.

Bardolph. Come in, woman!

Enter Mrs. Quickly

Quickly. By your leave; I cry you mercy: give your worship good morrow.

Falstaff. Take away these chalices. Go, brew me a pottle of sack finely.

Bardolph. With eggs, sir?

Falstaff. Simple of itself; I'll no pullet-sperm in my brewage. (*exit Bardolph.*) How now?

Quickly. Marry, sir, I come to your worship from Mistress Ford.

Falstaff. Mistress Ford? I have had ford enough; I was thrown into the ford; I have my belly full of ford.

Quickly. Alas the day! good heart, that was not her fault: she does so take on with her men; they mistook their erection.

Falstaff. So did I mine, to build upon a foolish woman's promise.

Quickly. Well, she laments, sir, for it, that it would yearn your heart to see it. Her husband goes this morning a-birding; she desires you once more to come to her, between eight and nine: I must carry her word quickly, she'll make you amends, I warrant you.

Falstaff. Well, I will visit her, tell her so; and bid her think what a man is: let her consider his frailty, and then judge of my merit.

Quickly. I will tell her.

Falstaff. Do so. Between nine and ten, sayst thou?

Quickly. Eight and nine, sir.

Falstaff. Well, be gone: I will not miss her.

Quickly. Peace be with you, sir.   *Exit*

Falstaff. I marvel I hear not of Master Brook; he sent me word to stay within: I like his money well.—By the mass, here he comes.

Enter Ford

Ford. God save you, sir!

Falstaff. Now, Master Brook,—you come to know what hath passed between me, and Ford's wife?

Ford. That, indeed, Sir John, is my business.

Falstaff. Master Brook, I will not lie to you, I was at her house the hour she appointed me.

Ford. And sped you, sir?

Falstaff. Very ill-favouredly, Master Brook.

Ford. How so, sir? Did she change her determination?

Falstaff. No, Master Brook; but the peaking Cornuto her husband, Master Brook, dwelling in a continual 'larum of jealousy, comes me in the instant of our encounter, after we had embrac'd, kiss'd, protested, and, as it were, spoke the prologue of our comedy; and at his heels, a rabble of his companions, thither provoked and instigated by his distemper, and (forsooth) to search his house for his wife's love.

Ford. What? While you were there?

Falstaff. While I was there.

Ford. And did he search for you, and could not find you?

Falstaff. You shall hear. As good luck would have it, comes in one Mistress Page, gives intelligence of Ford's approach; and in her invention, and Ford's wife's distraction, they convey'd me into a buck-basket.

Ford. A buck-basket?

Falstaff. By the Lord, a buck-basket!—ramm'd me in with foul shirts and smocks, socks, foul stockings, greasy napkins, that, Master Brook, there was the rankest compound of villanous smell, that ever offended nostril.

Ford. And how long lay you there?

Falstaff. Nay, you shall hear, Master Brook, what I have suffer'd, to bring this woman to evil, for your good. Being thus cramm'd in the basket, a couple of Ford's knaves, his hinds, were called forth by their mistress, to carry me in the name of foul clothes to Datchet-lane: they took me on their shoulders; met the jealous knave their master in the door; who ask'd them once or twice what they had in their basket: I quak'd for fear lest the lunatic knave would have search'd it; but fate (ordaining he should be a cuckold) held his hand. Well, on went he, for a search, and away went I for foul clothes. But mark the sequel, Master Brook: I suffered the pangs of three several deaths; first, an intolerable fright, to be detected with a jealous rotten bell-wether; next, to be compass'd like a good bilbo in the circumference of a peck, hilt to point, heel to head; and then, to be stopp'd in like a strong distillation with stinking clothes, that fretted in their own grease: think of that, a man of my kidney; think of that, that am as subject to heat as butter; a man of continual dissolution, and thaw: it was a miracle to 'scape suffocation. And in the height of this bath, when I was more than half stew'd in grease (like a Dutch dish) to be thrown into the Thames, and cool'd, glowing hot, in that surge, like a horse-shoe; think of that; hissing hot; think of that, Master Brook.

Ford. In good sadness, sir, I am sorry that for my sake you have suffer'd all this. My suit, then, is desperate; you'll undertake her no more?

Falstaff. Master Brook, I will be thrown into Etna, as I have been into Thames, ere I will leave her thus. Her husband is this morning gone a-birding: I have receiv'd from her another embassy of meeting; 'twixt eight and nine is the hour, Master Brook.

Ford. 'Tis past eight already, sir.

Falstaff. Is it? I will then address me to my appointment. Come to me at your convenient leisure, and you shall know how I speed; and the conclusion shall be crown'd with your enjoying her. Adieu. You shall have her, Master Brook; Master Brook, you shall cuckold Ford.   *Exit*

Ford. Hum! ha! is this a vision? is this a dream? do I sleep? Master Ford, awake! awake, Master Ford! there's a hole made in your best coat, Master Ford. This 'tis to be married! this 'tis to have linen, and buck-baskets! Well, I will proclaim myself what I am: I will now take the lecher; he is at my house; he cannot 'scape me; 'tis impossible he should; he cannot creep into a half-penny purse, nor into a pepper-box: but, lest the devil that guides him should aid him, I will search impossible places. Though what I am I cannot avoid, yet to be what I would not shall not make me tame: if I have horns, to make one mad, let the proverb go with me,—I'll be horn-mad.   *Exit*

Scene I

A street

Enter Mistress Page, Mistress Quickly, and William

Mrs. Page. Is he at Master Ford's already, think'st thou?

Quickly. Sure he is by this; or will be presently: but, truly, he is very courageous mad, about his throwing into the water. Mistress Ford desires you to come suddenly.

Mrs. Page. I'll be with her by and by: I'll but bring my young man here to school. Look where his master comes; 'tis a playing-day, I see.

Enter Sir Hugh Evans

How now, Sir Hugh, no school to-day?

Evans. No; Master Slender is let the boys leave to play.

Quickly. Blessing of his heart!

Mrs. Page. Sir Hugh, my husband says my son profits nothing in the world at his book. I pray you ask him some questions in his accidence.

Evans. Come hither, William; hold up your head; come.

Mrs. Page. Come on, sirrah; hold up your head; answer your master, be not afraid.

Evans. William, how many numbers is in nouns?

William. Two.

Quickly. Truly, I thought there had been one number more, because they say, 'Od's nouns.'

Evans. Peace your tattlings! What is 'fair,' William?

William. Pulcher.

Quickly. Polecats? there are fairer things than polecats, sure.

Evans. You are a very simplicity 'oman: I pray you peace. —What is *lapis*, William?

William. A stone.

Evans. And what is 'a stone,' William?

William. A pebble.

Evans. No; it is *lapis*: I pray you remember in your prain.

William. Lapis.

Evans. That is a good William. What is he, William, that does lend articles?

William. Articles are borrow'd of the pronoun; and be thus declin'd, *Singulariter, nominatiuo, hic, hæc, hoc.*

Evans. Nominatiuo, hig, hag, hog; pray you mark: *genitivo, huius.* Well, what is your accusative case?

William. Accusativo hinc.

Evans. I pray you, have your remembrance, child; *accusativo, hung, hang, hog.*

Quickly. 'Hang-hog' is Latin for bacon, I warrant you.

Evans. Leave your prabbles, 'oman.—What is the focative case, William?

William. O,—vocativo, O.

Evans. Remember, William; focative is *caret.*

Quickly. And that's a good root.

Evans. 'Oman, forbear.

Mrs. Page. Peace!

Evans. What is your genitive case plural, William?

William. Genitive case?

Evans. Ay.

William. Genitivo,—horum, harum, horum.

Quickly. Vengeance of Jinny's case! fie on her! never name her, child, if she be a whore.

Evans. For shame, 'oman.

Quickly. You do ill to teach the child such words: he teaches him to hick and to hack; which they'll do fast enough of themselves, and to call 'horum':—fie upon you!

Evans. 'Oman, art thou lunatics? hast thou no understandings for thy cases, and the numbers of the genders? Thou art as foolish Christian creatures as I would desires.

Mrs. Page. Prithee hold thy peace.

Evans. Show me now, William, some declensions of your pronouns.

William. Forsooth, I have forgot.

Evans. It is *qui, quæ, quod*: if you forget your 'quis,' your 'quæs,' and your 'quods,' you must be preeches. Go your ways and play, go.

Mrs. Page. He is a better scholar than I thought he was.

Evans. He is a good sprag memory. Farewell, Mistress Page.

Mrs. Page. Adieu, good Sir Hugh.   *Exit Sir Hugh*
Get you home, boy. Come, we stay too long.   *Exeunt*

Scene II

Enter Falstaff and Mistress Ford

Falstaff. Mistress Ford, your sorrow hath eaten up my suf-
ferance; I see you are obsequious in your love, and I pro-
fess requital to a hair's breadth, not only, Mistress Ford,
in the simple office of love, but in all the accoutrement,
complement, and ceremony of it. But are you sure of your
husband now?

Mrs. Ford. He's a-birding, sweet Sir John.

Mrs. Page. (within) What ho, gossip Ford! what ho!

Mrs. Ford. Step into the chamber, Sir John.   *Exit Falstaff*

Enter Mistress Page

Mrs. Page. How now, sweetheart? who's at home besides
yourself?

Mrs. Ford. Why, none but mine own people.

Mrs. Page. Indeed!

Mrs. Ford. No, certainly. *(aside to her)* Speak louder.

Mrs. Page. Truly, I am so glad you have nobody here.

Mrs. Ford. Why?

Mrs. Page. Why, woman, your husband is in his old lines
again: he so takes on yonder with my husband, so rails
against all married mankind; so curses all Eve's daugh-
ters, of what complexion soever; and so buffets himself
on the forehead, crying, 'Peer out, peer out!' that any
madness I ever yet beheld seem'd but tameness, civility,
and patience to this his distemper he is in now: I am glad
the fat knight is not here.

Mrs. Ford. Why, does he talk of him?

Mrs. Page. Of none but him, and swears he was carried out
the last time he search'd for him, in a basket; protests to
my husband he is now here, and hath drawn him and the

rest of their company from their sport, to make another experiment of his suspicion: but I am glad the knight is not here; now he shall see his own foolery.

Mrs. Ford. How near is he, Mistress Page?

Mrs. Page. Hard by, at street end; he will be here anon.

Mrs. Ford. I am undone, the knight is here.

Mrs. Page. Why then, you are utterly sham'd, and he's but a dead man. What a woman are you! Away with him, away with him! better shame, than murder.

Mrs. Ford. Which way should he go? how should I bestow him? Shall I put him into the basket again?

Re-enter Falstaff

Falstaff. No, I'll come no more i' the basket. May I not go out ere he come?

Mrs. Page. Alas, three of Master Ford's brothers watch the door with pistols, that none shall issue out; otherwise you might slip away ere he came. But what make you here?

Falstaff. What shall I do? I'll creep up into the chimney.

Mrs. Ford. There they always use to discharge their birding-pieces. Creep into the kiln-hole.

Falstaff. Where is it?

Mrs. Ford. He will seek there, on my word. Neither press, coffer, chest, trunk, well, vault, but he hath an abstract for the remembrance of such places, and goes to them by his note: there is no hiding you in the house.

Falstaff. I'll go out, then.

Mrs. Ford. If you go out in your own semblance, you die, Sir John, unless you go out disguis'd,—how might we disguise him?

Mrs. Page. Alas the day, I know not! There is no woman's gown big enough for him; otherwise he might put on a hat, a muffler, and a kerchief, and so escape.

Falstaff. For God's sake, devise something: any extremity, rather than a mischief.

Mrs. Ford. My maid's aunt, the fat woman of Brentford, has a gown above.

Mrs. Page. On my word, it will serve him; she's as big as he is: and there's her thrumm'd hat, and her muffler too. Run up, Sir John.

Mrs. Ford. Go, go, sweet Sir John: Mistress Page and I will look some linen for your head.

Mrs. Page. Quick, quick! we'll come dress you straight: put on the gown the while.   *Exit Falstaff*

Mrs. Ford. I would my husband would meet him in this shape: he cannot abide the old woman of Brentford; he swears she's a witch, forbade her my house, and hath threaten'd to beat her.

Mrs. Page. Heaven guide him to thy husband's cudgel; and the devil guide his cudgel afterwards!

Mrs. Ford. But is my husband coming?

Mrs. Page. Ay, in good sadness, is he, and talks of the basket too, howsoever he hath had intelligence.

Mrs. Ford. We'll try that; for I'll appoint my men to carry the basket again, to meet him at the door with it, as they did last time.

Mrs. Page. Nay, but he'll be here presently: let's go dress him like the witch of Brentford.

Mrs. Ford. I'll first direct my men, what they shall do with the basket. Go up, I'll bring linen for him straight.   *Exit*

Mrs. Page. Hang him, dishonest varlet! we cannot misuse him enough.

We'll leave a proof, by that which we will do,

Wives may be merry, and yet honest too:

We do not act that often jest and laugh,

'Tis old, but true, still swine eats all the draff.   *Exit*

Re-enter Mistress Ford with two Servants

Mrs. Ford. Go, sirs, take the basket again on your shoulders: your master is hard at door; if he bid you set it down, obey him: quickly, dispatch.   *Exit*

First Serv. Come, come, take it up.

Sec. Serv. Pray heaven it be not full of knight again.

First Serv. I hope not, I had as lief bear so much lead.

Enter Ford, Page, Shallow, Caius, and Sir Hugh Evans

Ford. Ay, but if it prove true, Master Page, have you any way then to unfool me again? Set down the basket, villain! Somebody call my wife. Youth in a basket! O you pandarly rascals, there's a knot; a ging, a pack, a conspiracy against me: now shall the devil be sham'd.—What, wife, I say! Come, come forth! Behold what honest clothes you send forth to bleaching!

Page. Why, this passes, Master Ford; you are not to go loose any longer, you must be pinion'd.

Evans. Why, this is lunatics! this is mad, as a mad dog!

Shallow. Indeed, Master Ford, this is not well, indeed.

Ford. So say I too, sir.

Re-enter Mistress Ford

Come hither, Mistress Ford, Mistress Ford, the honest woman, the modest wife, the virtuous creature, that hath the jealous fool to her husband! I suspect without cause, mistress, do I?

Mrs. Ford. Ay, God's my record, do you, if you suspect me in any dishonesty.

Ford. Well said, brazen-face! hold it out. Come forth, sirrah!
                                    Pulling clothes out of the basket

Page. This passes!

Mrs. Ford. Are you not asham'd? let the clothes alone.

Ford. I shall find you anon.

Evans. 'Tis unreasonable! Will you take up your wife's clothes? Come, away.

Ford. Empty the basket, I say!

Mrs. Ford. Why, man, why?

Ford. Master Page, as I am a man, there was one convey'd

out of my house yesterday in this basket: why may not he be there again? In my house I am sure he is: my intelligence is true, my jealousy is reasonable, pluck me out all the linen.

Mrs. Ford. If you find a man there, he shall die a flea's death.

Page. Here's no man.

Shallow. By my fidelity, this is not well, Master Ford; this wrongs you.

Evans. Master Ford, you must pray, and not follow the imaginations of your own heart: this is jealousies.

Ford. Well, he's not here I seek for.

Page. No, nor nowhere else but in your brain.

Ford. Help to search my house this one time. If I find not what I seek, show no colour for my extremity; let me for ever be your table-sport; let them say of me, 'As jealous as Ford, that searched a hollow walnut or his wife's leman.' Satisfy me once more, once more search with me.

Mrs. Ford. What, ho, Mistress Page! come you and the old woman down; my husband will come into the chamber.

Ford. Old woman? what old woman's that?

Mrs. Ford. Why, it is my maid's aunt of Brentford.

Ford. A witch, a quean, an old cozening quean! Have I not forbid her my house? She comes of errands, does she? We are simple men, we do not know what's brought to pass under the profession of fortune-telling. She works by charms, by spells, by the figure, and such daubery as this is, beyond our element: we know nothing. Come down, you witch, you hag, you, come down, I say!

Mrs. Ford. Nay, good sweet husband!—Good gentlemen, let him not strike the old woman.

Re-enter Falstaff in woman's clothes, and Mistress Page

Mrs. Page. Come, Mother Prat, come, give me your hand.

Ford. I'll prat her. (*Beating him*) Out of my door, you

witch, you rag, you baggage, you polecat, you ronyon!
out, out! I'll conjure you, I'll fortune-tell you.

Exit Falstaff

Mrs. Page. Are you not asham'd? I think you have kill'd the
poor woman.

Mrs. Ford. Nay, he will do it, 'tis a goodly credit for you.

Ford. Hang her, witch!

Evans. (aside) By yea and no, I think the 'oman is a witch
indeed: I like not when a 'oman has a great peard; I spy
a great peard under his muffler.

Ford. Will you follow, gentlemen? I beseech you, follow;
see but the issue of my jealousy: if I cry out thus upon
no trail, never trust me when I open again.

Page. Let's obey his humour a little further: come, gentlemen.   *Exeunt Ford, Page, Shallow, Caius, and Evans*

Mrs. Page. Trust me, he beat him most pitifully.

Mrs. Ford. Nay, by the mass, that he did not; he beat him
most unpitifully, methought.

Mrs. Page. I'll have the cudgel hallow'd, and hung o'er the
altar; it hath done meritorious service.

Mrs. Ford. What think you? may we, with the warrant of
womanhood, and the witness of a good conscience, pursue him with any further revenge?

Mrs. Page. The spirit of wantonness is sure scar'd out of him,
if the devil have him not in fee-simple, with fine and re-
covery, he will never, I think, in the way of waste, at-
tempt us again.

Mrs. Ford. Shall we tell our husbands how we have serv'd
him?

Mrs. Page. Yes, by all means; if it be but to scrape the figures
out of your husband's brains. If they can find in their
hearts the poor unvirtuous fat knight shall be any further
afflicted, we two will still be the ministers.

Mrs. Ford. I'll warrant they'll have him publicly sham'd,
and methinks there would be no period to the jest, should
he not be publicly sham'd.

Mrs. Page. Come, to the forge with it, then shape it: I would
not have things cool.   *Exeunt*

Scene III

A room in the Garter Inn

Enter Host and Bardolph

Bardolph. Sir, the Germans desire to have three of your
horses: the duke himself will be to-morrow at court, and
they are going to meet him.

Host. What duke should that be comes so secretly? I hear
not of him in the court. Let me speak with the gentlemen;
they speak English?

Bardolph. Ay, sir; I'll call them to you.

Host. They shall have my horses, but I'll make them pay;
I'll sauce them, they have had my house a week at command; I have turn'd away my other guests: they must
come off, I'll sauce them; come. *Exeunt*

Scene IV

A room in Ford's house

*Enter Page, Ford, Mistress Page, Mistress Ford,
and Sir Hugh Evans*

Evans. 'Tis one of the best discretions of a 'oman as ever I
did look upon.

Page. And did he send you both these letters at an instant?

Mrs. Page. Within a quarter of an hour.

Ford. Pardon me, wife. Henceforth do what thou wilt;
I rather will suspect the sun with cold
Than thee with wantonness: now doth thy honour stand,
In him that was of late an heretic,
As firm as faith.

Page.   'Tis well, 'tis well, no more:

> Be not as extreme in submission
> As in offence.
> But let our plot go forward: let our wives
> Yet once again, to make us public sport,
> Appoint a meeting with this old fat fellow,
> Where we may take him, and disgrace him for it.

Ford. There is no better way than that they spoke of.

Page. How? to send him word they'll meet him in the Park
at midnight? Fie, fie! he'll never come.

Evans. You say he has been thrown in the rivers; and has
been grievously peaten, as an old 'oman: methinks there
should be terrors in him, that he should not come; methinks his flesh is punish'd, he shall have no desires.

Page. So think I too.

Mrs. Ford. Devise but how you'll use him when he comes,
> And let us two devise to bring him thither.

Mrs. Page. There is an old tale goes, that Herne the hunter,
> Sometime a keeper here in Windsor forest,
> Doth all the winter-time, at still midnight,
> Walk round about an oak, with great ragg'd horns;
> And there he blasts the tree, and takes the cattle,
> And makes milch-kine yield blood, and shakes a chain
> In a most hideous and dreadful manner:
> You have heard of such a spirit, and well you know
> The superstitious idle-headed eld
> Receiv'd, and did deliver to our age,
> This tale of Herne the hunter, for a truth.

Page. Why, yet there want not many that do fear
> In deep of night to walk by this Herne's oak:
> But what of this?

Mrs. Ford.   Marry, this is our device,
> That Falstaff at that oak shall meet with us.
> [Disguis'd like Herne, with huge horns in his head.]

Page. Well, let it not be doubted but he'll come,
> And in this shape, when you have brought him thither,
> What shall be done with him? what is your plot?

Mrs. Page. That likewise have we thought upon, and thus:
Nan Page, my daughter, and my little son,
And three or four more of their growth, we'll dress
Like urchins, ouphs, and fairies, green and white,
With rounds of waxen tapers on their heads,
And rattles in their hands: upon a sudden,
As Falstaff, she, and I, are newly met,
Let them from forth a sawpit rush at once
With some diffused song: upon their sight,
We two in great amazedness will fly:
Then let them all encircle him about,
And fairy-like to pinch the unclean knight;
And ask him, why that hour of fairy revel,
In their so sacred paths, he dares to tread
In shape profane.

Mrs. Ford.　　　　And till he tell the truth,
Let the supposed fairies pinch him sound,
And burn him with their tapers.

Mrs. Page.　　　　　　　The truth being known,
We'll all present ourselves, dis-horn the spirit,
And mock him home to Windsor.

Ford.　　　　　　　The children must
Be practis'd well to this, or they'll ne'er do 't.

Evans. I will teach the children their behaviours; and I will
be like a jack-an-apes also, to burn the knight with my
taber.

Ford. That will be excellent; I'll go buy them vizards.

Mrs. Page. My Nan shall be the queen of all the fairies,
Finely attired in a robe of white.

Page. That silk will I go buy. (*aside*) And in that time.
Shall Master Slender steal my Nan away,
And marry her at Eton. Go, send to Falstaff straight.

Ford. Nay, I'll to him again in name of Brook:
He'll tell me all his purpose: sure he'll come.

Mrs. Page. Fear not you that. Go get us properties

And tricking for our fairies.

Evans. Let us about it, it is admirable pleasures and fery
   honest knaveries.   *Exeunt Page, Ford, and Evans*

Mrs. Page. Go, Mistress Ford,
   Send quickly to Sir John, to know his mind.

                                          Exit Mrs. Ford

I'll to the doctor, he hath my good will,
And none but he, to marry with Nan Page.
That Slender, though well landed, is an idiot;
And he my husband best of all affects.
The doctor is well money'd, and his friends
Potent at court: he, none but he, shall have her,
Though twenty thousand worthier come to crave her.

                                                 Exit

Scene V

The Garter Inn

Enter Host and Simple

Host. What wouldst thou have, boor? what, thickskin? speak, breathe, discuss; brief, short, quick, snap.

Simple. Marry, sir, I come to speak with Sir John Falstaff from Master Slender.

Host. There's his chamber, his house, his castle, his standing-bed and truckle-bed; 'tis painted about with the story of the Prodigal, fresh and new. Go, knock and call; he'll speak like an Anthropophaginian unto thee: knock, I say.

Simple. There's an old woman, a fat woman, gone up into his chamber: I'll be so bold as stay, sir, till she come down; I come to speak with her, indeed.

Host. Ha! a fat woman? the knight may be robb'd: I'll call.— Bully knight! bully Sir John! speak from thy lungs military: art thou there? it is thine host, thine Ephesian, calls.

Falstaff. (*above*) How now, mine host?

Host. Here's a Bohemian-Tartar tarries the coming down of thy fat woman. Let her descend, bully, let her descend; my chambers are honourable: fie! privacy? fie!

Enter Falstaff

Falstaff. There was, mine host, an old fat woman even now with me, but she's gone.

Simple. Pray you, sir, was 't not the wise woman of Brentford?

Falstaff. Ay, marry, was it, mussel-shell, what would you with her?

Simple. My master, sir, Master Slender, sent to her, seeing her go thorough the streets, to know, sir, whether one Nym, sir, that beguil'd him of a chain, had the chain or no.

Falstaff. I spake with the old woman about it.

Simple. And what says she, I pray, sir?

Falstaff. Marry, she says, that the very same man that beguil'd Master Slender of his chain, cozen'd him of it.

Simple. I would I could have spoken with the woman herself, I had other things to have spoken with her too, from him.

Falstaff. What are they? let us know.

Host. Ay, come, quick.

Simple. I may not conceal them, sir.

Host. Conceal them, or thou diest.

Simple. Why, sir, they were nothing but about Mistress Anne Page, to know if it were my master's fortune to have her, or no.

Falstaff. 'Tis, 'tis his fortune.

Simple. What, sir?

Falstaff. To have her, or no: go; say the woman told me so.

Simple. May I be bold to say so, sir?

Falstaff. Ay, tyke, who more bold?

Simple. I thank your worship: I shall make my master glad with these tidings.   *Exit*

Host. Thou art clerkly; thou art clerkly, Sir John. Was there a wise woman with thee?

Falstaff. Ay, that there was, mine host, one that hath taught me more wit than ever I learn'd before in my life; and I paid nothing for it neither, but was paid for my learning.

Enter Bardolph

Bardolph. Out, alas, sir! cozenage, mere cozenage!

Host. Where be my horses? speak well of them, varletto.

Bardolph. Run away with the cozeners: for so soon as I came beyond Eton, they threw me off, from behind one of them, in a slough of mire; and set spurs, and away; like three German devils; three Doctor Faustuses.

Host. They are gone but to meet the duke, villain: do not say they be fled; Germans are honest men.

Enter Sir Hugh Evans

Evans. Where is mine host?

Host. What is the matter, sir?

Evans. Have a care of your entertainments: there is a friend of mine come to town, tells me there is three cozen-germans, that has cozen'd all the hosts of Readins, of Maidenhead, of Colebrook, of horses and money. I tell you for good will, look you: you are wise, and full of gibes and vlouting-stocks, and 'tis not convenient you should be cozen'd. Fare you well.   *Exit*

Enter Doctor Caius

Caius. Vere is mine host de Jarteer?

Host. Here, master doctor, in perplexity, and doubtful dilemma.

Caius. I cannot tell vat is dat: but it is tell-a me dat you make grand reparation for a duke de Jamany: by my trot', dere is no duke dat the court is know, to come. I tell you for good vill: adieu.   *Exit*

Host. Hue and cry, villain, go! Assist me, knight, I am undone! Fly, run, hue and cry, villain! I am undone!

Exeunt Host and Bardolph

Falstaff. I would all the world might be cozen'd, for I have been cozen'd and beaten too. If it should come to the ear of the court, how I have been transform'd, and how my transformation hath been wash'd and cudgell'd, they would melt me out of my fat drop by drop, and liquor fishermen's boots with me: I warrant they would whip me their with fine wits, till I were as crest-fallen as a dried pear. I never prosper'd, since I forswore myself at primero. Well, if my wind were but long enough [to say my prayers], I would repent.

Enter Mistress Quickly

Now, whence come you?

Quickly. From the two parties, forsooth.

Falstaff. The devil take one party, and his dam the other! and so they shall be both bestow'd. I have suffer'd more for their sakes, more than the villanous inconstancy of man's disposition is able to bear.

Quickly. And have not they suffer'd? Yes, I warrant; spe-ciously one of them; Mistress Ford, good heart, is beaten black and blue, that you cannot see a white spot about her.

Falstaff. What tell'st thou me of black, and blue? I was beaten myself into all the colours of the rainbow; and I was like to be apprehended for the witch of Brentford, but that my admirable dexterity of wit, my counterfeiting the action of an old woman, deliver'd me, the knave con-stable had set me i' the stocks, i' the common stocks, for a witch.

Quickly. Sir, let me speak with you in your chamber, you shall hear how things go, and, I warrant, to your content. Here is a letter will say somewhat. Good hearts, what ado here is to bring you together! Sure, one of you does not serve heaven well, that you are so cross'd.

Falstaff. Come up into my chamber.   *Exeunt*

Scene VI

Enter Fenton and Host

Host. Master Fenton, talk not to me, my mind is heavy: I
    will give over all.
Fenton. Yet hear me speak. Assist me in my purpose,
    And (as I am a gentleman) I'll give thee
    A hundred pound in gold, more than your loss.
Host. I will hear you, Master Fenton, and I will (at the
    least) keep your counsel.
Fenton. From time to time I have acquainted you
    With the dear love I bear to fair Anne Page,
    Who, mutually, hath answer'd my affection,
    (So far forth as herself might be her chooser)
    Even to my wish: I have a letter from her
    Of such contents as you will wonder at;
    The mirth whereof, so larded with my matter,
    That neither singly can be manifested
    Without the show of both; fat Falstaff
    Hath a great scene: the image of the jest
    I'll show you here at large. Hark, good mine host.
    To-night at Herne's oak, just 'twixt twelve and one,
    Must my sweet Nan present the Fairy Queen;
    The purpose why, is here: in which disguise,
    While other jests are something rank on foot,
    Her father hath commanded her to slip
    Away with Slender, and with him at Eton
    Immediately to marry: she hath consented:
    Now, sir,
    Her mother (ever strong against that match
    And firm for Doctor Caius) hath appointed

That he shall likewise shuffle her away,
While other sports are tasking of their minds,
And at the deanery, where a priest attends,
Straight marry her: to this her mother's plot
She seemingly obedient likewise hath
Made promise to the doctor. Now, thus it rests:
Her father means she shall be all in white;
And in that habit, when Slender sees his time
To take her by the hand, and bid her go,
She shall go with him: her mother hath intended,
(The better to denote her to the doctor,
For they must all be mask'd, and vizarded)
That quaint in green she shall be loose enrob'd,
With ribands pendent, flaring 'bout her head;
And when the doctor spies his vantage ripe,
To pinch her by the hand, and on that token,
The maid hath given consent to go with him.

Host. Which means she to deceive? father, or mother?

Fenton. Both, my good host, to go along with me:
And here it rests, that you'll procure the vicar
To stay for me at church, 'twixt twelve and one,
And in the lawful name of marrying,
To give our hearts united ceremony.

Host. Well, husband your device; I'll to the vicar:
Bring you the maid, you shall not lack a priest.

Fenton. So shall I evermore be bound to thee;
Besides, I'll make a present recompence.   *Exeunt*

The Merry

...es of Windsor

Act V

Scene I

A room in the Garter Inn

Enter Falstaff and Mistress Quickly

Falstaff. Prithee no more prattling; go. I'll hold. This is the
third time; I hope good luck lies in odd numbers. Away!
go. They say there is divinity in odd numbers, either in
nativity, chance, or death. Away!

Quickly. I'll provide you a chain, and I'll do what I can to
get you a pair of horns.

Falstaff. Away, I say, time wears, hold up your head, and
mince.   *Exit Mrs. Quickly*

Enter Ford

How now, Master Brook? Master Brook, the matter will
be known to-night, or never. Be you in the Park about
midnight, at Herne's oak, and you shall see wonders.

Ford. Went you not to her yesterday, sir, as you told me
you had appointed?

Falstaff. I went to her, Master Brook, as you see, like a poor
old man, but I came from her, Master Brook, like a poor
old woman. That same knave, Ford her husband, hath
the finest mad devil of jealousy in him, Master Brook, that
ever govern'd frenzy. I will tell you, he beat me grievously, in the shape of a woman; for in the shape of man,
Master Brook, I fear not Goliath with a weaver's beam,

because I know also, life is a shuttle. I am in haste, go
along with me, I'll tell you all, Master Brook. Since I
pluck'd geese, play'd truant, and whipp'd top, I knew not
what 'twas to be beaten, till lately. Follow me, I'll tell you
strange things of this knave Ford, on whom to-night I
will be reveng'd, and I will deliver his wife into your
hand. Follow; strange things in hand, Master Brook!
Follow.   *Exeunt*

Scene II

Windsor Park

Enter Page, Shallow, and Slender

Page. Come, come; we'll couch i' the castle-ditch, till we see the light of our fairies. Remember, son Slender, my daughter.

Slender. Ay, forsooth, I have spoke with her, and we have a nay-word, how to know one another: I come to her in white, and cry, 'mum;' she cries 'budget,' and by that we know one another.

Shallow. That's good too: but what needs either your 'mum,' or her 'budget?' the white will decipher her well enough. It hath struck ten o'clock.

Page. The night is dark, light and spirits will become it well. Heaven prosper our sport! No man means evil but the devil, and we shall know him by his horns. Let's away; follow me.   *Exeunt*

Scene III

Enter Mistress Page, Mistress Ford, and Doctor Caius

Mrs. Page. Master Doctor, my daughter is in green: when you see your time, take her by the hand, away with her to the deanery, and dispatch it quickly: go before into the Park: we two must go together.

Caius. I know vat I have to do, adieu.

Mrs. Page. Fare you well, sir. (*exit Caius.*) My husband will not rejoice so much at the abuse of Falstaff, as he will chafe at the doctor's marrying my daughter: but 'tis no matter; better a little chiding, than a great deal of heart-break.

Mrs. Ford. Where is Nan now? and her troop of fairies? and the Welsh devil?

Mrs. Page. They are all crouch'd in a pit hard by Herne's oak, with obscur'd lights; which, at the very instant of Falstaff's and our meeting, they will at once display to the night.

Mrs. Ford. That cannot choose but amaze him.

Mrs. Page. If he be not amaz'd, he will be mock'd; if he be amaz'd, he will every way be mock'd.

Mrs. Ford. We'll betray him finely.

Mrs. Page. Against such lewdsters, and their lechery,
  Those that betray them do no treachery.

Mrs. Ford. The hour draws on. To the oak, to the oak!

Exeunt

Scene IV

Enter Sir Hugh Evans disguised, with others as Fairies

Evans. Trib, trib, fairies; come; and remember your parts: be pold, I pray you, follow me into the pit, and when I give the watch-'ords, do as I pid you: come, come, trib, trib.

Exeunt

Scene V

Enter Falstaff disguised as Herne

Falstaff. The Windsor bell hath struck twelve; the minute draws on. Now, the hot-blooded gods assist me! Remember, Jove, thou wast a bull for thy Europa, love set on thy horns. O powerful love, that, in some respects, makes a beast a man; in some other, a man a beast. You were also, Jupiter, a swan, for the love of Leda. O omnipotent Love, how near the god drew to the complexion of a goose! A fault done first in the form of a beast;—O Jove, a beastly fault! And then another fault, in the semblance of a fowl; —think on 't, Jove; a foul fault! When gods have hot backs, what shall poor men do? For me, I am here a Windsor stag, and the fattest, I think, i' the forest. Send me a cool rut-time, Jove, or who can blame me to piss my tallow?—Who comes here? my doe?

Enter Mistress Ford and Mistress Page

Mrs. Ford. Sir John! art thou there, my deer? my male deer?

Falstaff. My doe, with the black scut? Let the sky rain potatoes; let it thunder to the tune of Green Sleeves, hail kissing-comfits, and snow eringoes; let there come a tempest of provocation, I will shelter me here.

Mrs. Ford. Mistress Page is come with me, sweetheart.

Falstaff. Divide me like a brib'd buck, each a haunch: I will keep my sides to myself, my shoulders for the fellow of this walk; and my horns I bequeath your husbands. Am I a woodman, ha? Speak I like Herne the hunter? Why, now is Cupid a child of conscience, he makes restitution. As I am a true spirit, welcome!   *Noise within*

Mrs. Page. Alas, what noise?

Mrs. Ford. Heaven forgive our sins!

Falstaff. What should this be?

Mrs. Ford.⎫
Mrs. Page.⎬ Away, away!   *They run off*

Falstaff. I think the devil will not have me damn'd, lest the oil that's in me should set hell on fire; he would never else cross me thus.

Enter Sir Hugh Evans, disguised as before; Pistol, as Hobgoblin; Mistress Quickly, Anne Page, and others, as Fairies, with tapers

Quickly. Fairies, black, grey, green, and white,
    You moonshine revellers, and shades of night,
    You orphan heirs of fixed destiny,
    Attend your office, and your quality.
    Crier Hobgoblin, make the fairy oyes.
Pistol. Elves, list your names; silence, you airy toys.
    Cricket, to Windsor chimneys shalt thou leap;
    Where fires thou find'st unrak'd, and hearths unswept,
    There pinch the maids as blue as bilberry,
    Our radiant queen hates sluts, and sluttery.
Falstaff. They are fairies; he that speaks to them shall die:
    I'll wink, and couch: no man their works must eye.
                        Lies down upon his face
Evans. Where's Bede? Go you, and where you find a maid
    That ere she sleep has thrice her prayers said,
    Raise up the organs of her fantasy,
    Sleep she as sound as careless infancy,
    But those as sleep, and think not on their sins,
    Pinch them, arms, legs, backs, shoulders, sides, and shins.
Quickly. About, about;
    Search Windsor Castle, elves, within, and out:
    Strew good luck, ouphs, on every sacred room;
    That it may stand till the perpetual doom,
    In state as wholesome as in state 'tis fit,
    Worthy the owner, and the owner it.
    The several chairs of order look you scour
    With juice of balm, and every precious flower:
    Each fair instalment, coat, and several crest,
    With loyal blazon, evermore be blest!
    And nightly, meadow-fairies, look you sing,
    Like to the Garter's compass, in a ring:
    Th' expressure that it bears, green let it be,
    More fertile-fresh than all the field to see;
    And *Honi soit qui mal y pense* write
    In emerald tufts, flowers purple, blue, and white;
    Like sapphire, pearl, and rich embroidery,

Buckled below fair knighthood's bending knee:
Fairies use flowers for their charactery.
Away, disperse: but till 'tis one o'clock,
Our dance of custom, round about the oak
Of Herne the hunter, let us not forget.

Evans. Pray you lock hand in hand; yourselves in order set;
And twenty glow-worms shall our lanterns be,
To guide our measure round about the tree.
But, stay, I smell a man of middle-earth.

Falstaff. Heavens defend me from that Welsh fairy, lest he
transform me to a piece of cheese!

Pistol. Vile worm, thou wast o'erlook'd even in thy birth.

Quickly. With trial-fire touch me his finger-end:
If he be chaste, the flame will back descend,
And turn him to no pain; but if he start,
It is the flesh of a corrupted heart.

Pistol. A trial, come.

Evans.   Come; will this wood take fire?

                    They burn him with their tapers

Falstaff. Oh, Oh, Oh!

Quickly. Corrupt, corrupt, and tainted in desire!
About him, fairies, sing a scornful rhyme,
And as you trip, still pinch him to your time.

SONG

Fie on sinful fantasy!
Fie on lust, and luxury!
Lust is but a bloody fire,
Kindled with unchaste desire,
Fed in heart, whose flames aspire,
As thoughts do blow them higher and higher.
Pinch him, fairies, mutually;
Pinch him for his villany;
Pinch him, and burn him, and turn him about,
Till candles, and starlight, and moonshine be out.

During this song they pinch Falstaff. Doctor Caius comes one

way, and steals away a boy in green; Slender another way, and
takes off a boy in white; and Fenton comes, and steals away
Mistress Anne Page. A noise of hunting is heard within. All the
Fairies run away. Falstaff pulls off his buck's head, and rises

Enter Page, Ford, Mistress Page, and Mistress Ford

Page. Nay, do not fly, I think we have watch'd you now:
Will none but Herne the hunter serve your turn?
Mrs. Page. I pray you, come, hold up the jest no higher.
Now, good Sir John, how like you Windsor wives?
See you these, husband? do not these fair yokes
Become the forest better than the town?
Ford. Now, sir, who's a cuckold now? Master Brook, Fal-
staff's a knave, a cuckoldy knave, here are his horns, Mas-
ter Brook: and, Master Brook, he hath enjoy'd nothing
of Ford's but his buck-basket, his cudgel, and twenty
pounds of money, which must be paid to Master Brook;
his horses are arrested for it, Master Brook.
Mrs. Ford. Sir John, we have had ill luck; we could never
meet. I will never take you for my love again, but I will
always count you my deer.
Falstaff. I do begin to perceive that I am made an ass.
Ford. Ay, and an ox too: both the proofs are extant.
Falstaff. And these are not fairies: I was three or four times
in the thought they were not fairies, and yet the guiltiness
of my mind, the sudden surprise of my powers, drove the
grossness of the foppery into a receiv'd belief, in despite
of the teeth of all rhyme and reason, that they were fairies. See now how wit may be made a Jack-a-Lent, when
'tis upon ill employment!
Evans. Sir John Falstaff, serve Got, and leave your desires,
and fairies will not pinse you.
Ford. Well said, fairy Hugh.
Evans. And leave you your jealousies too, I pray you.
Ford. I will never mistrust my wife again, till thou art able
to woo her in good English.

Falstaff. Have I laid my brain in the sun, and dried it, that it wants matter to prevent so gross o'erreaching as this? Am I ridden with a Welsh goat too? shall I have a coxcomb of frieze? 'Tis time I were chok'd with a piece of toasted cheese.

Evans. Seese is not good to give putter; your pelly is all putter.

Falstaff. 'Seese' and 'putter'? Have I liv'd to stand at the taunt of one that makes fritters of English? This is enough to be the decay of lust and late-walking through the realm.

Mrs. Page. Why, Sir John, do you think, though we would have thrust virtue out of our hearts by the head and shoulders, and have given ourselves without scruple to hell, that ever the devil could have made you our delight?

Ford. What, a hodge-pudding? a bag of flax?

Mrs. Page. A puff'd man?

Page. Old, cold, wither'd, and of intolerable entrails?

Ford. And one that is as slanderous as Satan?

Page. And as poor as Job?

Ford. And as wicked as his wife?

Evans. And given to fornications, and to taverns, and sack, and wine, and metheglins, and to drinkings, and swearings, and starings? pribbles and prabbles?

Falstaff. Well, I am your theme: you have the start of me, I am dejected; I am not able to answer the Welsh flannel: ignorance itself is a plummet o'er me: use me as you will.

Ford. Marry, sir, we'll bring you to Windsor, to one Master Brook, that you have cozen'd of money, to whom you should have been a pandar: over and above that you have suffer'd, I think, to repay that money will be a biting affliction.

Page. Yet be cheerful, knight: thou shalt eat a posset tonight at my house, where I will desire thee to laugh at my wife, that now laughs at thee: tell her Master Slender hath married her daughter.

Mrs. Page. (*aside*) Doctors doubt that: if Anne Page be my daughter, she is, by this, Doctor Caius' wife.

Enter Slender

Slender. Whoa, ho! ho, father Page!

Page. Son, how now? how now, son? have you dispatch'd?

Slender. Dispatched? I'll make the best in Gloucestershire know on 't: would I were hang'd, la, else!

Page. Of what, son?

Slender. I came yonder at Eton to marry Mistress Anne Page, and she's a great lubberly boy. If it had not been i' the church, I would have swing'd him, or he should have swing'd me. If I did not think it had been Anne Page, would I might never stir!—and 'tis a postmaster's boy.

Page. Upon my life, then, you took the wrong.

Slender. What need you tell me that? I think so, when I took a boy for a girl. If I had been married to him, for all he was in woman's apparel, I would not have had him.

Page. Why, this is your own folly, did not I tell you how you should know my daughter, by her garments?

Slender. I went to her in white, and cried 'mum,' and she cried 'budget,' as Anne and I had appointed, and yet it was not Anne, but a postmaster's boy.

Mrs. Page. Good George, be not angry, I knew of your purpose; turn'd my daughter into green; and, indeed, she is now with the doctor at the deanery, and there married.

Enter Caius

Caius. Vere is Mistress Page? By gar, I am cozen'd: I ha' married un garçon, a boy; un paysan, by gar: a boy, it is not Anne Page, by gar, I am cozen'd.

Mrs. Page. Why, did you take her in green?

Caius. Ay, be gar, and 'tis a boy: be gar, I'll raise all Windsor.   *Exit*

Ford. This is strange. Who hath got the right Anne?

Page. My heart misgives me:—here comes Master Fenton.

Enter Fenton and Anne Page

How now, Master Fenton?

Anne. Pardon, good father; good my mother, pardon!

Page. Now, mistress; how chance you went not with Master
   Slender?

Mrs. Page. Why went you not with master doctor, maid?

Fenton. You do amaze her: hear the truth of it.
   You would have married her most shamefully,
   Where there was no proportion held in love.
   The truth is, she and I, long since contracted,
   Are now so sure that nothing can dissolve us.
   The offence is holy that she hath committed,
   And this deceit loses the name of craft,
   Of disobedience, or unduteous title,
   Since therein she doth evitate and shun
   A thousand irreligious cursed hours,
   Which forced marriage would have brought upon her.

Ford. Stand not amaz'd, here is no remedy:
   In love, the heavens themselves do guide the state,
   Money buys lands, and wives are sold by fate.

Falstaff. I am glad, though you have ta'en a special stand
   To strike at me, that your arrow hath glanc'd.

Page. Well, what remedy? Fenton, heaven give thee joy!
   What cannot be eschew'd must be embrac'd.

Falstaff. When night-dogs run, all sorts of deer are chas'd.

Mrs. Page. Well, I will muse no further. Master Fenton,
   Heaven give you many, many merry days!
   Good husband, let us every one go home,
   And laugh this sport o'er by a country fire,
   Sir John and all.

Ford.   Let it be so. Sir John,
   To Master Brook you yet shall hold your word,
   For he, to night, shall lie with Mistress Ford.   *Exeunt*

(*Appended is the conclusion, as given in Q, correspond-ing to ll. 219—end of F.*)

[*Mrs. Ford.* Come, Mistress Page, I will be bold with you,
　'Tis pity to part love that is so true.
Mrs. Page. Although that I have miss'd in my intent,
　Yet I am glad my husband's match was cross'd;
　Here, Master Fenton, take her, and God give thee joy.
Evans. Come, Master Page, you must needs agree.
Ford. I' faith, sir, come, you see your wife's well pleas'd.
Page. I cannot tell, and yet my heart 's well eas'd,
　And yet it doth me good the doctor miss'd.
　Come hither, Fenton, and come hither, daughter;
　Go to, you might have stay'd for my good will,
　But since your choice is made of one you love,
　Here take her, Fenton, and both happy prove.
Evans. I will also dance and eat plums at your weddings.
Ford. All parties pleas'd, now let us in to feast,
　And laugh at Slender, and the doctor's jest.
　He hath got the maiden, each of you a boy
　To wait upon you, so God give you joy;
　And, Sir John Falstaff, now shall you keep your word,
　For Brook this night shall lie with Mistress Ford.]